HANGMAN'S BRAE

Crime and Punishment in and around Bygone Aberdeen

Norman Adams

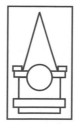

**TOLBOOTH
BOOKS**
Banchory, Scotland

First published 1993 by
TOLBOOTH BOOKS

The Spinney, Auchattie, Banchory,
Kincardineshire AB31 3PT

ISBN 0 9521738 0 8
British Library Cataloguing-in-Publication Data.
A catalogue record for this book is available
from the British Library.

Typeset by Bryan Angus, Aberdeen.
Printed by Dave Barr Print, Glasgow.

Contemporary drawing of Castlehill, Aberdeen, in 1830, showing Hangman's Brae (left) with 'Hangman's Hoose'. Note the swinging sign with symbol of hanged man. (Author's Collection).

Contents

Prologue

Skull-Duggery?

A yellowing skull unearthed in a mass grave of medieval human skeletons in Aberdeen in 1981 bore the hallmark of violent crime.

The skull of an unknown man had a triangular-shaped hole in the top right-hand side caused be a severe blow to the head with a blunt instrument.

Experts from Aberdeen University's Department of Anatomy in Marischal College, concluded the man had suffered a depressed fracture, but the blow had not been fatal. The terrible wound healed.

This early crime came to light when more than 126 skeletons of men, women and children, dating from the 14th century, were excavated at the site of an ancient Carmelite Friary in the Green, an early focus of life in Aberdeen.

How did the victim come by his injury? Who was responsible? Did he fall or was he pushed? The answers are lost forever.

But one other intriguing question for the armchair criminologist: Was the punctured skull first-ever tangible proof of a mugging or attempted murder in bygone Bon-Accord?

Sadly, the catalogue of crime grew bloodier in Aberdeen and round about. But the perpetrators could expect little or no mercy.

Norman Adams 1993

Chapter One

'Facing Down Marischal Street'

'Carryin' great loads the Shore up frae,
by Marischal Street and Hangman's Brae'.
- John Smith (1830).

A street map of Aberdeen is a guide to the darker side of the city's history.

Stroll down the granite bow of Justice Street and you are on the trail of witches burned at the stake. Climb the Gallowgate and you follow the road that led to the gibbet.

In Correction Wynd stood the House of Correction where inmates were ruled with a rod of iron.

Thieves' Port, Gallowhill Croft, Heading Hill and Hangman's Brae are names, some colloquial, well kent in the past but no longer with us. They evoke an age when justice was swift and bloody.

How did it all come about?

The judicial system in Scotland was the brainchild of King David I, who reigned from 1124 to 1153.

Aberdeen was created a royal burgh by the king and only rich burgesses had a voice in public affairs. These guardians of law and local customs were forerunners of today's town councillors.

In the reign of William the Lion (1165 - 1214), who granted the burgh its earliest extant charter around 1179, there is mention of a Sheriff in Aberdeen.

Ancient charters chiefly dealt with matters of trade, but burgesses were responsible for legal matters.

In medieval Aberdeen royal courts of justice - 'Heid Courtis' - were held at Heading Hill. In October 1394 King Robert III granted a charter which sanctioned the building of a tolbooth and courthouse.

Surviving parchments of a burgh court record - 1317 - the oldest yet to be found in Scotland, gives details of three cases of

7

'wrang et unlaw', involving two cases of defamation and a wrangle over land.

Although early records deal mainly with the civil actions we know that in 1399 Marioth Fethes was banished from the burgh for two years for reset and theft. As a result of committing assault on several occasions Elena Scotcok was banished for 100 years and a day!

At the turn of the 14th century, Paul Crab, probably a descendant of John Crab, whose name lives on in Craibstone Street, Aberdeen, sued a fellow burgess and his own brother.

By 1405 fixed penalties were incurred - assault by sword, axe, knife or stick cost eight shillings. Assault with a fist, four shillings. At this time burgesses were responsible for 'watch and ward' - whereby persons who overstepped the law would voluntarily commit themselves to jail and not walk free until the law was satisfied. In Paisley, law-breakers themselves fetched the key of the tolbooth!

In bygone Scotland a fortified entrance to a town was called a 'port' - and Aberdeen had several, including the Justice Port at the North-east corner of the Gallowgate.

Justice Street derives its name from Justice Port, or 'Thieves' Port', where dismembered limbs of criminals were spiked. The street led to one of the earliest known execution sites in Aberdeen - the 'Heiding Hill', Heading Hill, where, quite literally, condemned persons were 'heidit' - beheaded. This was accomplished with a heavy two-handed sword but later a primitive guillotine, 'The Maiden', was used.

In a green hollow between Heading Hill and Castle Hill the circuit courts dealt with justice in the open air. Here in the late 16th century witches were executed and during 'The Trubles' one of Lord Sinclair's soldiers was shot by firing squad for murder.

The road to the Gallow Hills ran from the Justice Port, along Park Road, towards the Links and the Bridge of Don. The south end of the road to the gibbet may still be seen turning to the left at Urquhart Place after crossing the bridge over the single-track railway line.

The 'Thieves' Brig', referred to as Pons Latronum in medieval records, bridged the Powcreek Burn, in line with present-day Jasmine Terrace. In 1604 William Findlay, a local builder, was paid £3 6s 8d for helping to repair the 'Theiwes Brigis'.

The gibbet was erected on a grassy-topped knoll, known to a

generation of football fans as 'The Misers' Hillie', because of the free view it provided of matches at nearby Pittodrie Stadium, home of Aberdeen Football Club. On old maps the place is referred to as the Gallow Hills.

This airy spot could also be reached by the Gallow Port and across marshland where lepers lodged and worshipped St Anna, their patron saint. However, James Gordon's famous map of Aberdeen in 1661, pinpoints 'Gallowgate Hill', to the north side of the line of Spring Garden, so it is likely executions were also carried out at Porthill. Gallowgate is designed 'Via Furcarum' in ancient Latin charters. It means 'Thief Gate'.

Until 1776 criminals in Aberdeen were executed and hung in chains at Gallow Hill, at the top of Errol Street, *pour encourager les autres.*

Gibbeting or hanging in chains of corpses of executed criminals was a common occurrence in the British Isles, and according to the chronicler Holinshed the culprit was sometimes hanged alive in chains to die of exposure and starvation on the gibbet.

A gallows stood at the Links during the 16th century, and four pirates were hanged on specially-erected gibbets at Footdee Blockhouse in 1597.

Old Aberdeen had its own place of execution - at Tillydrone, on land owned and controlled by the Bishops. They had power to put thieves and other lawbreakers to death, but their influence was restricted.

To the south-west of Aberdeen a gibbet stood 'at the crossing of the roads on the lands of Rudriston', near the Bridge of Dee. A Jacobite robber and army deserter, James Davidson, a native of Brechin, lifted some of the gloom of his execution on the first day of July 1748 by wearing a tartan vest and breeches, white stockings, tied with blue garters, clean shirt, white gloves and a white cap tied with blue ribbons. His escort of St. George's Dragoons also wore their best dress, with orange cockades to commemorate the Battle of the Boyne.

Criminals were hanged, burned and drowned, the sentences carried out in the most public place so as to deter others. In Aberdeen official drowning took place in a grim pool in the harbour opposite Shore Brae, known as 'The Pottie'. Six persons, two men convicted of murder, and four women convicted of child murder, suffered this terrible fate between the years 1584 and 1587. The condemned person was simply bound hand and foot and thrown into the water.

When plague was rife in 1585 the Town Council acted swiftly against any citizen giving food or shelter to a stranger... 'the man to be hangit and the woman to be drownit'. Two women who defied the burghers were banished instead.

The main arena for capital punishment in Aberdeen over the centuries was the Castlegate, at one time a wide-open market place dominated by 'The Mids o' Mar', the Tolbooth.

Executions were carried out in the heart of the city until 1857, when John Booth became the last person to be publicly hanged in Aberdeen. He walked onto the scaffold platform, via an upstairs window in the old Town House in Castle Street, at a point 20 yards west of the Lodge Walk pend. During the last century 18 persons (17 men and one woman) were publicly hanged in Aberdeen.

In the last century a hanging stane - a big stone with a cavity for the end of the upright beam of the gallows - was unearthed at the former Castle Street site of the Duke of Gordon's statue, now in Golden Square. This may have been the site of the old 'Market Place' gallows of the 18th century. The last person to hang there was William Webster, thief and housebreaker, in June 1787.

More than 30 years ago a stone fitting the same description was dug up a few yards to the east of Lodge Walk by workmen lifting the old tram lines. A local historian arranged for a marker to be set in the 'cassies' but the site vanished during road improvements until a sharp-eyed schoolboy noticed its disappearance.

In June 1788 a new scaffold was erected outside the Tolbooth for the execution of James Grant, shopbreaker and thief.

The proximity of the gallows at the spot gave rise to a grim Aberdeen saying - a warning that a person would end their days 'facing down Marischal Street', the brae that plunges towards the harbour from the Castlegate. (In Glasgow they had a similar dire insult: 'You'll die facing the Monument!' - the condemned hanged in front of the South Prison could clearly see Nelson's Monument on Glasgow Green).

Scan a street map of oil boom Aberdeen and you'll find no trace of Hangman's Brae.

The steep hill, a popular spot during bygone icy winters for youngsters seeking a thrilling 'slide', vanished in 1857 when it became part of the broader and more convenient Castle Terrace, leading to the docks and Footdee.

The brae, originally the Futty Wynd and later named Castle Brae, sloped towards James Street.

The common hangman lived in Hangman's Brae in a house dubbed, 'Hangman's Hoose'. A nearby bridge which spanned the old Aberdeen - Port Elphinstone Canal was called 'Hangman's Brig'. It was replaced with the 'Tarrie Briggie'.

A drawing of Castlehill in 1830 clearly shows 'Hangman's Hoose', complete with a swinging signboard, with a match-stick figure of a hanged man.

The hangman finished off the work begun by the policeman. In its early days Aberdeen was served by a part-time police force. The Justice Court Book of 1657 sets out their instructions. They had to arrest on sight all suspicious night walkers, all vagabonds, all idle sturdy beggars, gypsies and report for prosecution Sabbath breakers, fornicators and whoremongers, drunks and even children who disobeyed their parents.

Policing of a kind was in existence over the next century or so but an increase in crime resulted in the formation of a far more permanent force. By 1818 Town Sergeants kept the peace during daylight hours while a new force of 24 night watchmen patrolled streets armed with cudgels and carrying lanterns. Their uniform was purely functional, consisting of a Tam o' Shanter bonnet and a stout coat, buttoned at the neck and reaching the ankles. They were universally known as 'Charlies', after Charles the First in whose reign the police system was reorganised in earlier times.

By 1829 the Town Sergeants, who had for so long jealously guarded their peace-keeping role, lost out to a regular Day Patrole of hand-picked night watchmen.

The new-style force had 42 regulations to comply with and had to deal with all sorts, ranging from hardened criminals to less offensive ballad singers and graffiti artists, depending on your viewpoint.

Aberdeen's first regular police station stood on the south side of Castle Street. In 1820 the night watchmen moved from the old guardhouse to Huxter Row, later swept away when the present Town House was built. Moves to the old Records Office in Castle Street, Concert Court and Lodge Walk followed.

Today the nerve centre of Grampian Police Force is in Queen Street, a stone's throw from its roots.

11

Chapter Two

Johnny Milne o' Tillyskukie

The quaintly-named farm of Tillyskukie - Gaelic for 'Hill of the Clumsy Shape' - on the north slope of the Corse Burn on the fringe of Deeside and Donside has a link with Aberdeen's most despised public servant, the common hangman.

The history of capital punishment shows that in the early days executioners were selected from a class of people who had barely escaped the scaffold or transportation.

The chronicles have left us the names of a few of the Aberdeen executioners - John Justice, James Chapman, Robbie Welsh, Jock McDonald and John Scott.

But the best known of an infamous breed was Johnny Milne.

What is Johnny's connection with Tillyskukie, a 90-acre farm which marches cheek by jowl with Corse House, a private nursing home, and the picturesque ruin of Corse Castle, built in 1581 by William Forbes? It seems Johnny worked at Tillyskukie - the name first appeared in the 1696 Aberdeenshire Poll Book as Tillyskuk - at the turn of the last century.

In 1806 he stole beehives at Corse and was hauled up before the magistrates. He was sentenced to seven years' transportation to the colonies but escaped by applying for the job of the Aberdeen hangman. The previous holder of the post, Jock McDonald, had been dead for a year and the town was having difficulty in finding a successor. Johnny Milne got the job and was paid £7 10 shillings for a half year's salary to October 1, 1806.

Johnny had an evil streak and after being appointed Aberdeen's official executioner he returned to his old haunts.

He was given a frosty welcome at Tillyskukie and sought lodgings elsewhere for the night. At Tillyorn, the farm next door to Tillyskukie, he was again shown the door. But the farmer at Tillyorn did not trust the hangman and he and a good neighbour kept watch till dawn should Johnny seek revenge by burning the farm buildings.

Johnny Milne's first execution in his new post was almost his last.

The culprit was Andrew Hosack, caught red-handed after robbing a cottage at Rubislaw in August 1809. Hosack had gained entry by the chimney but as he escaped with several articles of clothing a watch-dog raised the alarm.

Neighbours chased Hosack into a cornfield where he was cornered with stolen items in his possession. When his house was searched other stolen goods were retrieved.

When he was tried in April 1810 he appeared under his assumed name of Andrew Fraser. He was found guilty of housebreaking and theft and was sentenced to death.

Sinister rumours swept Aberdeen and neighbourhood while he awaited his execution on June 15. Hosack was blamed for the brutal murder of Banffshire man George Milne and his daughter Margaret at Upper Auchanasie, near Keith, in January 1797. After they were hacked to death with an axe their home was ransacked then torched. A reward of 100 guineas had failed to find the culprit.

Hosack was attended in jail by Rev Charles Gordon, who helped him draw up a declaration of innocence of the Milne murders. It was signed by Hosack the day before his walk to the gallows.

The stoutly-built Hosack, who was 56, repeated his innocence on the scaffold and died 'penitently'.

But there was a touch of black comedy about the affair. It had been arranged Hosack's corpse would be transported by cart from Castle Street to the Gallow Hill for burial. But every effort to hire a cart failed. Attempts were made by the civil powers to secure transport from coalmen on the quay, but these were thwarted by the carters and some seamen. It seemed no one was willing to lend or hire out a cart of horse for the purpose of carrying the grim load.

As Johnny Milne performed the last of his duties at the scaffold his horse and cart were 'borrowed'. His daughter was manhandled as she tried to stop the hijacking by her father's employers.

When news reached his ears he appealed to the sympathy of the crowd against the 'indignities which had been offered to himself and his daughter'.

He then formally resigned on the spot to the wild cheers of the spectators. It is unclear who cut down Hosack's corpse as Johnny staged his one-man 'strike'.

Hosack's body was eventually buried in a shallow grave at

Gallow Hill, but during the night it was stolen by surgeons.

Johnny Milne had second thoughts and was persuaded that night to carry on his role as common hangman.

Johnny was no shadowy figure. He carried out menial tasks around the burgh when not hanging or whipping felons in public.

He appears in a famous print of bygone Aberdeen - Seaton's 'View of Castle Street', dated 1806, the year Johnny took up his new job.

He is the squat, unkempt figure seen talking to a fishwife. A Tam o' Shanter bonnet is pulled down over his grey straggly hair. He is also wearing a heavy coat and has a walking stick under his arm. Hands that found far grimmer work hold a fat fish. For the hangman's perks included one fish out of every creel on market day and one peat out of every cart.

Johnny, his wife Christian Waters, and their family lived in a small, isolated house in Hangman's Brae.

Christian, it seems, strayed to the wrong side of the law after her husband's death. In less than a year she appeared three times in Aberdeen Police Court on charges of breaking the peace in the neighbourhood of their former home.

In October 1831 the 'Aberdeen Journal' reported tersely: 'Christian Waters, or Milne, relict of the late hangman, was once more brought before the Police Court on Wednesday charged with committing a breach of the peace at Hangman's Brae, and breaking a pane of glass in the house of her husband's successor. She was sent 60 days to Bridewell'.

The same punishment had been meted out after previous offences.

The newspaper does not name Johnny's successor, but he could have been John Scott, former assistant hangman in Edinburgh. Scott was hired by Aberdeen Town Council to hang Catherine Humphrey in 1830. Scott, who eventually became the Edinburgh hangman, was described in the records of that city in July 1835 as 'late executioner at Aberdeen'.

The reasons behind Christian Milne's tantrums are unclear, but perhaps she had a score to settle with the new hangman?

In previous centuries the burgh hangman was a man of mystery.

When the Town Council appointed John Justice to the post on February 18, 1596, they had previously experienced great difficulty in retaining a public executioner in Aberdeen. Criminals,

14

they reluctantly admitted, had gone unpunished because there was no one suitable to enforce death, banishment, scourging, branding or torture.

It seems when they did recruit someone to take on the grisly job he would be hounded out of office - and the town - by mobs 'of the meanest and simplest sort', throwing insults and stones, causing him injury and the burghers great embarrassment.

The council took the step of appointing John Justice, whose name was probably a pseudonym. A proclamation at the Market Cross warned that any person, no matter their sex or age, who forced the new hangman to quit his office by offending him by word or deed, would be severely punished.

Justice, who was to play a bloody role in the execution of the witches, occupied a 'little house' under the stair of the Tolbooth. It would appear the house was in a state of disrepair at the time, for the council agreed to fix the door and provided a lock for it. John Justice was paid 6s 8d for every witch he executed.

A Fyvie robber, Alexander Cheyne, was hanged in Aberdeen in September 1748, after a brief respite, by James Chapman. At one time the hangman pronounced doom on the culprit and was known as the doomster or dempster. This bleak ceremony was abolished in 1733 when clerks took over the job of reading the death sentence on the gallows.

In Aberdeen in 1770 - 71 an anonymous executioner was paid 6s 8d per month and 15s a year, representing the rent of a house that went with the job. These sums were paid by the Burgh Treasurer, the Dean of Guild forked out an additional £2 14s in lieu of clothes.

By November 1773 the Town Council advertised for a new hangman, as the job had been vacant for some time.

The post was soon filled by Robert Welsh, who within a few weeks of his new appointment asked, and received, an increase in his salary - his new wage was 13s 4d a month.

Welsh was still in office in 1800 - 01 when his total emolument was £12 7s.

The last man to be hanged by him was a brother of the celebrated Peter Young, the gypsy robber.

John Young stabbed to death a member of his gang at Chapel of Garioch, but, despite extenuating circumstances, he was sentenced to hang. A plot to free Young from the Tolbooth was foiled and the culprit faced Welsh in December 1801.

As the hangman approached with the condemned man's shroud, a chilling sight indeed, Young drew back in horror and said he 'didn't like to hae that creature Robbie Welsh's hands about him'.

Young's courage faltered again as he was led from the Laigh Tolbooth and his eyes fell on the coffin, or 'shell' as it was known, which would be used to transport his body to the anatomists after Robbie Welsh finally got his hands on him.

In 1803 - 04 Welsh was succeeded part way through the year by John McDonald. He died round about the end of March 1805 without ever carrying out a hanging.

Scottish hangmen did not dandify their position by wearing top hats, breeches and silk stockings, or highly-coloured garb, as favoured by their European brethren.

Their mode of dress was plain, although Thomas Askern of York, a convicted prisoner who hanged the Ratho murderer in Edinburgh in 1864, was dressed like 'a rat catcher'.

Edinburgh's 'lockman' wore livery of white and grey cloth. Masks were sometimes worn to protect identity. A hooded medical student beheaded the bodies of the Scottish insurrections John Baird and Andrew Hardie after they were hanged before the court house in Stirling in August 1820. At a later execution in the same town the hangman wore a black wig, and was disguised.

In May 1835 a mysterious hangman was hired by Dundee, who had no official executioner for 15 years, to dispatch an Irish weaver.

A link with Aberdeen's public hangman can still be seen today. For some years the red-padded chair, made locally in the Queen Anne style, was in every day use in the Town Sergeant's office in Aberdeen Town House. It has since been moved to the former council chamber. It was acquired by Robert Welsh from East Church of St Nicholas and later inherited by Johnny Milne, who is said to have occupied it while watching the condemned man on the eve of his execution.

The office of common hangman was abolished by act of the Town Council on January 27, 1834. His dwelling in 'Hangman's Brae' was later put up for sale. The decision to abolish the post was taken the previous November when councillors decided it was cheaper to hire the services of an executioner from out of town.

Chapter Three

Heads and Grisly Tales!

On the scaffold, Sir Walter Raleigh thumbed the cruel edge of the executioner's axe and said wryly: 'This is a sharp medicine, but it will cure all diseases'.

No one knows how often the Aberdeen headsman administered his special brand of 'sharp medicine' on Heading Hill, but we know the method of execution by sword or axe became obsolete in the burgh during the 16th century.

Sir John Gordon, whose father the Earl of Huntly dropped dead at the Battle of Corrichie, near Banchory, in October 1562, was captured and taken to Aberdeen where he 'wis headit on thi heidin' hill'.

Mary, Queen of Scots, according to legend, was forced to watch Huntly's third son walk to the scaffold. A contemporary report suggests the condemned man was 'shockingly mangled by the axe of an unskilled executioner'.

It had been suggested the unfortunate Sir John was a victim of 'The Maiden', the Scottish forerunner to the guillotine, but it is more likely his botched execution led to its introduction in the far north.

The Scottish 'Maiden' - it can be seen in the Museum of Antiquities in Queen Street, Edinburgh - was first used in the Scottish capital on April 3, 1566. Its victim was Thomas Scott, under secretary of Perth, for his part in the murder of the Queen's favourite, David Riccio, at Holyrood.

The wooden frame of the machine resembles a painter's easel and is about 10 feet high. Heads dropped into buckram sacks.

Two years earlier when Edinburgh's much-wielded beheading sword became worn out William Macartney sold his own two-handed sword for 'ane heiding sword' for £2 to the magistrates.

There is a popular error that the Regent Morton invented 'The Maiden', also called 'The Widow', and was the first person to suffer by it.

But a decapitating machine was employed in Ireland in the

14th century and in Germany in the 1520s. The only place in England to have a beheading machine was Halifax - hence the old Yorkshire saying, 'From Hell, Hull and Halifax, good Lord deliver us'. Morton saw this machine in action.

Sir John Gordon of Haddo was beheaded by 'The Maiden' in Edinburgh in 1644, after being held a prisoner in 'Haddo's Hole' in St Giles. The Edinburgh 'Maiden' was last used in 1710.

The crude, chopping blade of the Aberdeen 'Maiden' is exhibited at Provost Skene's House in Aberdeen.

There is mention of 'The Maiden' in the Aberdeen Treasurer's Accounts for 1594 - 95. George Annand was hired to transport the machine to Heading Hill and back again for safe-keeping at the Earl Marischal's house in the Castlegate. He also carried out some repairs and maintenance, including sharpening the axe and greasing the rope on which it was suspended. Thus: 'Item, for ane garrone to the madin, mending of her be George Annand, wright scharping the aix, for saip to the tow, kareing of hir to the hill, and hame agane to my Lord Merschells cloiss - 25 shillings'.

Two men were executed on this occasion. The Dean of Guild Accounts explain: 'Item, for upputting of ane scaffol, and dountacking thairof, at the executioun of Douglas and Litster - 6s 8d'. Annand's efforts also earned him a quart of ale at a cost of 2s 8d to the burgh.

The Aberdeen 'Maiden' last tasted human blood in 1615 when Francis Hay was beheaded for the murder of Adam Gordon, brother of the Laird of Gight.

A curious punishment involving amputation was earmarked for the Castlegate in 1640 after George Leslie assaulted the young Laird of Tolquhon. The Earl Marischal ordered the attacker's right hand to be chopped off and a small scaffold was erected at the Market Cross. A last minute reprieve by the Master of Forbes saved the day - and Leslie's hand.

Hanging was believed to be a form of execution for the lower classes. While the 'Cock of the North's' son was honourably 'heidit' in Aberdeen five of his followers were hanged.

The early gallows was provided by nature - the bough of a tree. The victim was simply hoisted into the air at the end of a rope to die slowly of strangulation. The Gallows Tree o' Mar, between Braemar and Inverey, is a grim reminder of the time when the local laird had absolute power over his subjects.

Centuries before the measured drop of Victorian hangmen, a

condemned person climbed a ladder propped against the gallows beam and stood on a rung while the executioner adjusted the noose. Then the hangman pushed the culprit off the ladder. He would sometimes pull on his legs to hurry the criminal's departure from this world.

The method of hanging had not changed much by the time they led cattle thief and housebreaker John Hutcheon to the gallows in Aberdeen in June 1765. After praying for a short while and reading a Bible, Hutcheon was 'thrown off' and his corpse later acquired by the surgeons.

Eleven years later the method of hanging had altered slightly for the execution of Alexander Morison, the last man to be hung in chains at the Gallow Hill at Pittodrie. Morison, a respected cartwright, murdered his wife with an axe in their Guestrow home. She took 12 days to die. A huge crowd defied stormy conditions to watch the execution (In 1801 they braved a terrible snowstorm to see Welsh hang the caird, John Young).

Morison, wearing a jaunty red nightcap and matching waistcoat, was conveyed to the gallows in a horse-drawn cart, accompanied by the hangman, Robbie Welsh. The cap, or hood, masked the dying man's facial contortions.

A graphic description of Morison's execution tells how his feet were bound; the noose adjusted around his neck. Then the horse was whipped in order to pull the cart from under the murderer's feet.

Death was a slow process, even with the introduction of the 'horse and cart' method. The leap from a ladder often broke the felon's neck. In 1758 Aberdeen invalid James Paterson hanged himself in a Tolbooth cell rather than face the hangman. He ingeniously used his crutch and a rope plaited from straw. He was 'stiff and cold' when found.

Improvements in technique were instigated, ranging from the rope itself to the double-leaved trapdoor, which instantly launched the culprit into eternity. The 'double flap door' was introduced by the Government during the time of William Calcraft, public executioner from 1829 to 1874, who was hired by Aberdeen Town Council to perform the last three public executions in the city.

Early in his career Calcraft would go beneath the gallows to 'draw the bolt' supporting a collapsible platform. But later a lever was enough to release the trapdoor. The Victorian long drop was designed to cause instantaneous death by severing the cervical vertebrae.

A legend persists that Deacon Brodie, a prototype Jekyll and Hyde, was first to suffer upon the new drop which he himself designed. When shopbreaker James Grant was executed in Aberdeen in June 1788 it was reported he had died on 'the drop invented by the famous Mr Brodie'. Not so. Brodie, in fact, was executed for robbery in Edinburgh four months later. And he certainly did not construct Auld Reekie's new 'movable platform for the execution of criminals'.

Criminals were hanged individually or in batches. Multiple hangings took place in Aberdeen, with a triple execution in Castle Street on May 23, 1823. The culprits were Thomas Donaldson, his accomplice William Buchanan, and William Macleod, who were found guilty at the High Court of Justiciary on charges of theft and stouthrief (robbery with violence).

Donaldson, Buchanan and a third man, William Duncan, committed the offences in Cuminestown, near Turriff. The latter was transported 'beyond the seas for life'.

After they had robbed a lone woman in her home at Greenhill of Auchiries Macleod and his brother, who was also transported for life, left a trail of footprints in the snow for the Sheriff's Officer to follow.

The three men showed remarkable courage on the scaffold. After shaking hands with each other they embraced three clergymen individually. Buchanan volunteered to take the handkerchief with which to signal the hangman. 'At twenty minutes past three the drop fell, and this world closed on them forever', wrote a reporter. Their bodies were cut down and carried to the Gallow Hill and buried in a freshly-dug grave.

Two murderers who were hanged together - the first double execution in Aberdeen for 70 years - made bizarre history when they walked to the scaffold on May 22, 1822. Robert Mackintosh of Crathie and William Gordon, Aberdeen wife killer, refused to wear shrouds and were each dressed in black. A week before the executions the pair had made a fruitless escape attempt from the Tolbooth. Mackintosh's aged father made a vain journey to London to try and get remission of that part of Lord Gillies' sentence which ordered his body to be handed over for dissection. He failed. To add insult to injury, after their corpses were given to the surgeons, Mackintosh's skeleton was exhibited in the university's anatomy department museum.

A man and a woman were the first persons to be hung in chains at Gallow Hill - on November 24, 1752.

Seaman William Wast was found guilty of murder and was joined at the scaffold by Christian Phren, a farm servant. Phren had murdered her illegitimate child and then tried to conceal the crime by burning the body.

After her arrest in Aberdeenshire the unhappy woman was forced to travel to Aberdeen with the charred remains of the bairn in her apron.

Wast, in good spirits despite his fate, offered to put the rope around his neck. 'He died hard, as the sea phrase is', commented the 'Aberdeen Journal'. Phren's body was taken down and given to the surgeons. Wast's corpse hung till his bones were bleached by the sea breezes he had once loved. Years later his skeleton was stolen and dumped in the doorway of a Methodist meeting house in Queen Street, Aberdeen.

Pinned to its breastbone was a label on which was scrawled an amusing couplet:

I, William Wast, at the point of damnation,
Request the prayers of this congregation'.

By winter 1766 it was improper to hang a woman in chains in Aberdeen. Mrs. Keith and her son William were imprisoned at Banff accused of strangling her husband ten years before! Despite the passage of time, and some judicial irregularities at their Circuit Court trial in Aberdeen, the perpetrators of the Northfield Murder were found guilty. They were fed on a diet of bread and water in their cells at the Tolbooth before being hanged on separate days. Mrs. Keith's body was anatomized while her son's was hung in chains at Gallow Hill.

After Alexander Morison became the last man to be hung in chains in Aberdeen, on Friday, November 1, 1776, his friends stole his body for burial and dumped the chains in the street. In time the chains, and the burgh stocks, which were kept for safety in St Mary's Chapel below the East Church of St Nicholas, were obtained by a local building contractor.

The bodies of executed criminals which escaped the anatomist's knife were sometimes buried at the foot of the Aberdeen gibbet. About a century ago when new foundations were dug at the city's powder magazine at Gallow Hill a number of human skeletons were found.

In later years further excavations by quarrymen of the dry, sandy soil revealed a number of thick chains. A first it was thought they had been used to bind gibbeted corpses. But the chains were in fact lightning conductors associated with the former powder magazine, removed from the site in the interests of safety. (Hanging in chains was abolished in Britain in 1834).

Heretics, traitors and witches suffered at the stake. In Aberdeen the 'awfu' reek and stink o' the burnings hung over the burgh for days after the notorious witch executions in the late 16th century.

The sentence pronounced on a witch by the 'doomster' was that she be 'virreit' at the stake until she be dead and 'thaireftir brint in asches'.

On the day of the execution the witch was tied to the stake, piled high with an assortment of flammable debris - trees, peat, coal and barrels soaked with tar and oil. The executioner strangled her with a rope before smoke and flames enveloped the terrible scene. But things did go wrong. A woman murderer was 'literally burnt alive' at Tyburn in 1726 when the executioner loosened his grip on the rope when flames scorched his flesh.

The last person to be burned to death in Aberdeen suffered at the stake in 1647, after being found guilty of bestiality.

Through the ages drowning, stoning, boiling alive, throwing from rocks and pressing with heavy weights were the chief methods of capital punishment in the British Isles.

Hanged, drawn and quartered was a punishment reserved for traitors. After his execution in Edinburgh in May 1650 Montrose's dismembered right arm was sent to Aberdeen. It was still on display on a pinnacle above the Tolbooth when King Charles II passed through the town from Speymouth. The offending limb was removed and interred in the Mither Kirk for 11 years. After the Reformation it was placed in a coffin draped with crimson velvet and solemnly handed back to the Grahams, and act which earned the council 'manie heartie thanks' from Montrose's son.

Scourging, the cuckstool, the jougs, the hairshirt and branding were some of the punishments reserved for minor crimes. Transportation was handed out for a number of offences. Sometimes persons 'cheated the widdie' - escaped hanging - and were sent instead to plantations in North America or the West Indies.

Two jailers who guarded the man executed for bestiality in

Aberdeen were described as 'scorgeris'.

The burgh's whipping stations were situated at three places in the 18th century - the Bow Brig, which spanned the Denburn at the Green, the head of Sir John's Wynd and at the Tolbooth stair-head.

In 1771 a barber's apprentice, Adam Frain, appeared before the Sheriff charged with breaking into the house of town advocate John Durno and stealing books and banknotes. He was publicly whipped by the common hangman - first at the Tolbooth stair-head and then at the Bow Brig. He was jailed and banished from Aberdeenshire for life. He was warned if he ever set foot in the county again he would be 'apprehended, incarcerated, whipt, and again banished'. Adam Frain was 13 years old.

Yet John Davidson, a miller at Gordon's Mills, Tillydrone, escaped with only a public whipping after stabbing his wife in 1765. And Thomas Scotchie, who played the drums for a puppet show, received the same punishment for attempting to ravish Barbara Wilson on the road to the Kirk of Slains.

In 1749 James Aberdein was jailed for four months and publicly whipped through the streets by the hangman on the last Friday of four successive months. His crime? Cutting down a tree in a Hilton estate.

Military justice was particularly brutal. Joshua Smith, a private whose regiment was garrisoned in Aberdeen in 1752, suffered 800 lashes for theft. One would hope they were not inflicted all at once.

In April 1766 six persons - four soldiers and two civilians - were indicted for stealing meal from a ship berthed at Banff. Three were found guilty and sentenced to be whipped through the streets of Aberdeen and banished to the plantations for life. Friday the 13th proved an unlucky day for the hangman. He had no sooner started the punishment when he was attacked by a mob. The hangman and a military escort were beaten and bruised by flying stones and clubs and the three culprits escaped. No arrests were made and they got clean away, even though a reward of 20 guineas was offered for their recapture.

The ducking-stool stood in the south-west corner of Castle Street from the early 14th century. It consisted of a long timber beam, evenly balanced on a pivot, with a small chair at one end. The malefactor was strapped to the chair and the burgh hangman, once in position at the other end of the beam, would dip his prisoner in and out of the 'thief's pottie' at will.

Two hundred years ago 'ducking at the cran' was a common punishment handed out for minor offences. Women, deemed immoral by the Kirk, were the chief sufferers. The cran was used for loading and unloading heavy goods from ships at the harbour, and was stored in a shed in James Street.

In July 1638 a woman suffered the indignity of being ducked in the harbour and whipped once a week.

The Aberdeen Observer reported: 'On 1 July 1638 a frail female was sentenced by the Kirk Session 'to be cartit from the mercat croce to the Kayheid, thair to be dowked at the cran, and thereafter to be put in the correction hous, quhaill she shall remain till whitsunday nixt (July 1638 to May 1639) and to be qulipped everie Monday during that space'.

In 17th century Aberdeen the Church moved against slanderers and backbiters by placing them in the cuckstool.

In 1405 an Aberdeen byelaw ruled that anyone abusing the baillies of the burgh or any king's officer would 'kiss the cuckstool'. For a second offence the offender would be placed in the cuckstool and be fouled with eggs, dung and suchlike. A third offence would result in the offender being banished from the burgh for a year and a day.

Branks - an iron bridle and gag - and jougs - a hinged iron collar attached to a gibbet post or a kirk wall - were public punishments confined to gossips, nagging wives and women with a 'flyting and evil toung'.

The stocks was used both in town and country. The Courtbook of Leys, kept by Sir Thomas Burnett, the first Baronet of Leys, and still in existence at Crathes Castle, records how in 1623 James Paterson was sentenced to 24 hours in the Banchory stocks for 'borrowin' a horse, while another villain was dealt with for 'picklocking ane house'.

Bizarre modes of punishment were inflicted. In 1770, fire-raisers Christian Spence and her son James Gray were carried through Aberdeen in a cart, with ropes about their necks, with the hangman in attendance.

Gray was banished from Scotland for life while his mother was given a short jail sentence.

The public hangman was also present in 1759 when three thieves and resetters, all females, were forced to stand bareheaded for one hour at the Aberdeen Market Cross, with notices of their crimes pinned to their breasts and a noose around their necks. Jail and banishment for life followed.

Aberdeen's first printer, Edward Raban, the self-styled 'The Laird of Letters', who had a workshop off the Castlegate in the 17th century, had a contract with the Town Council to print the papers which were 'prined on the bristis' of culprits pilloried at the scaffold.

As a printer perhaps he was familiar with some of the quaint words which vividly described the criminals, gallowbirds, destined for the gibbet - crackraip, gallow-breid, minker or hempie, and, of course, the executioner, referred to in the olden days as the basar, burrio, lockman of hangie.

Colloquial terms for upholders of the law in Scotland ranged from writer chiel or man of business (lawyer) to sugarallie hat and tarrie hat (policeman). The latter insult was usually hurled at an Aberdeen bobby from a safe distance!

'Facing down Marischal Street'. Worm's-eye view of the 'Hanging Stane' in Castle Street, Aberdeen.

Hangman's Brae - Edinburgh-style. Illustration of Aberdeen
executions are rare. This etching by James Skene of Rubislaw
shows the Grassmarket gallows. (From Grant's 'Old and New Edinburgh').

Chapter Four

The Aberdeen Witch Report

High inside the west tower of Aberdeen's Flemish-style Town House the Charter Room houses a curious set of ancient documents.

They make blood-chilling reading.

The faithful record, kept by Dean of Guild, William Dun, in the late 16th century, lists the cost of executing witches in the burgh during a brief, but horrific spell of blood-letting.

The expense of buying loads of coal, peat, timber and other items such as tar barrels and the stake, plus dressing and setting it, are carefully noted in ink, comprised of oak gall and iron fillings.

The cost of food and drink, shackles and locks for the hapless prisoners was also taken into account. Even the hangman's fee. John Justice was paid £1 6s 8d for executing four witches in one day.

Altogether 23 women and one young man, the son of a witch, were convicted, strangled then burned at Heading Hill during the year 1596 - 97. There could have been more.

John Skelton wrote of the period: 'From the Moray Firth to Berwick the reek of tar barrels and faggots darkened the air'.

The Dean of Guild, who had also zealously organised the hanging of four pirates at Footdee, was rewarded with the sum of £47 3s 4d for his 'extraordinary pains' in the burning of a great number of witches.

The suffering of the poor wretches who died in the name of superstition and ignorance is incalculable and beyond belief.

His sacred Majesty, King James the Sixth of Scotland and First of England, must bear some of the burden for their barbaric treatment. He had a deep-rooted fear of witches and would later write a bestseller on witchcraft, 'Daemonologie', a commentary on the Biblical text: 'Thou Shalt Not Suffer a Witch to Live'.

The woman-hating king's loathing intensified in 1590 when he personally examined the North Berwick witches at their trial in

Holyrood Palace in Edinburgh.

The warlock, Dr Fian, alias John Cunningham, a schoolmaster from Saltpans in the Lothians, was hideously tortured during the trial. Dr Fian and his witches were accused of raising a storm in an attempt to wreck the ship carrying King James and his new bride, Anne, Princess of Denmark, home to Scotland.

The ship, Nicholas, was furnished in the town of Aberdeen, crewed by local men, and captained by a future Provost, John Collinson. James was a popular monarch with Aberdonians, presenting the town with charters and visiting it on occasions.

Aberdeen's first witch-burning took place on June 16, 1590, when Barbara Card was 'burnt on hedownis hill' - a bloody omen! A witch was burned a few years later for the burgh accounts carry this item: 'For the barrellis, fyre, petties, and towis, witht ane staik, to execute and burne the witche that wes burnt, £3 10s'.

Because the High Court of Justiciary could not keep pace with the fanatical king's vengeance the monarch hit on the idea of appointing Royal Commissions throughout Scotland to deal with witches without further formality. In a single day 14 Commissions were granted.

In February 1596 a Royal Commission was granted in favour of the Provost and Baillies of the burgh of Aberdeen for the arrest and trial of persons suspected of witchcraft. The king's signature on this important document sealed the fate of the North-east's witches.

In the coming months the king's agents went about their task with sickening gusto and soon the 'dittays' - charges - were mounting against alleged witches in Aberdeen, Buchan, Deeside and Banffshire.

The Aberdeen Coven, under the leadership of Thomas Leys, whose mother Janet Wishart was a leading light, held their nocturnal gillatrypes at the Mercat Cross and Fish Cross in the Castlegate or nearby tree-ringed St Katherine's Hill, in the area of present-day Adelphi.

The Deeside witches chose a less public spot - the forbidding Hill of Craiglash, a broomstick's ride from Torphins and Kincardine o' Neil. There, at the Warlock Stone, a grey granite boulder located on the northern slope of the hill, the coven kept appointments with Auld Nick. In the 16th century the 'Gryt Stane o' Craigleauche' stood in an open space, but today it is dwarfed by tall pines. The stone is damaged, broken in two. It may have been the work of superstitious farmfolk or the law, fearing a resurgence of the witch cult.

Witchcraft in North-east Scotland had its roots in pagan times, when our ancestors worshipped the gods of nature. Early Christianity did not destroy the ancient ways, nor did the Reformation. Although the Kirk remained the cornerstone of life, folk sometimes sought solace from the spirits of the forest, lofty peaks and secret places in the face of death, famine and other disasters.

Until the middle of the last century farmers still believed in the tradition of Goodman's Croft, the practice of leaving untilled and uncropped land as a peace offering to the devil. The De'il's Faulie, Clootie's Croft or Halie Man's Rigs were some of the other names given to this bit of scrubland.

Witches were feared, yet important, members of the community. They could work 'weel as well as woe'. They would cure a sick child, heal cattle or make sure of a good harvest for a farmer or fisherman. Some witches traded in winds - to guide a sailor safely home to port or to winnow corn after it had been cut.

Written charms carried by a patient could cure toothache. Witches intervened in domestic feuds or a business arrangement.

A gibbet was a source of 'hackit flesh' for witches to work their magic. A culprit's hand - the Hand of Glory - was much prized. Burglars turned it into a burning torch believing it induced sleep on their victims.

The Aberdeen witchcraft trials indicate that the gallows at the Links was visited by local witches and their servants at midnight. Janet Wishart was accused of forcing John Taylor's wife to accompany her to the gallows where 'ane deid mann being hinging thair, baid hir hald his futt, quhill thow cuttit af a pairt of all his members'. The grim experience proved too much for Mrs Taylor who fainted. She was ordered by Janet to keep her silence - or else!

Revenge was swift, and sometimes fatal, if a witch was slighted.

Stabler John Pyet lay dying in his house in Aberdeen's Justice Port because Janet Wishart failed to get her hands on his property, a piece of land. The archives describe how Pyet lay in bed for 18 weeks, continually melting away like a white candle, and burning as if he were in a fiery oven.

Everything from curses, the evil eye, to 'diverse writings', was used to work woe.

The Deeside witch Helen Rogie was accused of murdering her

enemies by roasting their wax images in a fire. When arrested Rogie had in her possession a 'pictour' - a lead image of a man used as a mould.

The common man was not entirely helpless against evil charms. A cross of rowan, bound with red thread, was said to 'put witches to their speed'. Holly and honeysuckle also proved strong protection.

One bizarre method of protection was to 'score abune the breath'. A person struck down by witchcraft could remove the spell by carving a cross on the witch's forehead with a silver pin. It happened in Braemar.

As the bloody stain of the great witch hunts spread throughout Scotland in the late 16th century neighbour turned against neighbour, and many innocent people stood accused. It seemed no one was safe from malicious gossip. No matter your place in society or the passage of time. But you had to choose your words carefully on occasions. Marjorie Mearns begged forgiveness in a church after slandering an Aberdeen widow by calling her a witch. Marjorie had to grovel on her knees before the widow and congregation and utter the words: 'Tongue, you lied, tongue, you lied'.

In the North-east the accused witches and warlocks were rounded up by their local laird and brought to the Tolbooth in Aberdeen to face trial. We know this because an item in the Dean of Guild Accounts reads: 'For peittis and coillis to try thame in the librarie tua dayes befoir the executioun - 6s 8d'. The above entry begs the questions: - What was the purpose of the peat and coals? To kindle the library fire to keep the magistrates warm? Or to heat John Justice's branding irons?

Torture was commonplace at witchcraft trials and John Justice's 'job description' included 'tormenting' prisoners. The Aberdeen witches were branded on the cheek.

Weird confessions were extracted from the alleged witches. Flesh and bone and a person's spirit were soon crushed by implements of torture, such as the red-hot irons, the pilliewinkis and thumbikins (thumbscrews), the torkas (pincers) or cashielaws. The North Berwick warlock Dr. Fian had needles thrust under his finger nails which were then torn out by pincers. His legs were crushed to pulp by the 'torment of the boots' - wedges were hammered between the boot and the victim's naked leg. Unable to walk he was carted off to the execution place at the Castle Hill in Edinburgh.

At least two of the Aberdeen witches died in captivity. The accounts note that Suppack, alias Helen Mackenzie, died in prison and it cost 6s 8d to bury her. Isobel Monteith cheated John Justice by hanging herself in jail. But her corpse was trailed through the streets of the burgh in a cart and buried for a fee of 10 shillings.

The executions drew a large proportion of Aberdeen's entire population of around 7,500. There was a huge turn-out for the execution of a Lumphanan witch, Margaret Clerk or Bain, who had been taught the Black Arts at 15 by her sister who had been burned as a witch in Edinburgh.

A wooden crush barrier failed to control the mob of spectators and two spars were smashed. Repairs cost the burgh 8s 8d. A spar was broken at the execution of four Deeside witches. Thomas Dickson's halberd - a long-staffed pole mounted with a spear head axe blade - was also broken during an execution and he received £1 10 shillings as recompense.

This is an extract from the Accounts of the Dean of Guild concerning Margaret Clerk's execution which took place after her trial on March 25, 1597:-

> Item: for sexteine laidis of peittis to hir, £1 15s.
> Item: for four lead of fir, 16s.
> Item: for ane oylie barrell, 10s.
> Item: for ane tar barrell, 6s 8d.
> Item: for tua irne barrellis, 6s 8d.
> Item: for thrie fadone of tow, 3s.
> Item: for the staik, careing and dressing it, 13s 4d.
> Item: for the careing of the peattis, coillis, and barrellis, to the hill, 8s.
> Item: for the careing of four sparris to withstand the preas of pepill, quhairof thair was tua brokin, 8s 8d.
> Item: for Jon Justice for his fie, 6s 8d.

The public hangman enjoyed rich pickings. After dispatching Janet Douglas and Agnes Smellie for a fee of 13s 4d, John Justice earned himself an extra 6s 8d for burying two thieves at the foot of the Heading Hill gallows at the same time.

Coal used for the burnings was stored at St Ninian's Chapel at Castle Hill.

The total expense of lodging the witches in the Tolbooth and their subsequent executions came to £177 17s 4d.

Louise B. Taylor, writing in 1942 of the Aberdeen witch trials, has this to say:

'For the most part the unfortunate wretches mentioned had certainly very little to do with annoyances attributed to their evil spirits - the bringing of a murrain upon cattle, the blighting of crops, and so on; but to their superstitious neighbours they served as an outlet for their hurt and bewildered vengeance.

'These Devil's Agents, in other words, were made the scapegoats for acts the people of the time hesitated to ascribe to the Lord, but in which they could not see the penalty from their own ignorance and laziness'.

Witchcraft trials in the North-east did not end with the 16th century. In 1626 Walter Baird confessed in Aberdeen to the crime of having a conversation with the devil. In 1630 Marion Hendry appeared before the Bishop of Aberdeen on witchcraft charges.

Aberdeen's Dean of Guild Accounts for 1626-27 itemizes the hire of a barrow 'to carry the crippell witches, 6s'. Andrew Clark earned £6 13s 4d for 'his paynes' in writing out the charges against the witches, and for acting as clerk at the court hearings. Alex Ramsay received £142 3s 4d for upkeep of the witches, whose prospects must have been bleak indeed, although we have no details of their fate.

The civic records of Aberdeen are the most complete in Scotland, with the earliest extant charter granted by King William the Lion around 1179.

But there is a tragic omission in the contemporary history of the Aberdeen witchcraft trials of the 16th century. The Charter Room contains the original Dean of Guild Accounts. The charter, manners and various pursuits of our burghal forefathers make interesting reading.

But, apart from a few worm-eaten, fragile pages, there is no trace whatsoever of the original records of the trials. They have disappeared. Handwritten markings and notes in the margins of the pages suggested they were the actual copies used in court against the accused persons.

The records were lost for years but in the middle of the last century they were discovered among papers belonging to the town of Aberdeen. The Spalding Club, which took its name from Aberdeen's first historian John Spalding, borrowed the records for transcription and eventual inclusion in Volume One of the Miscellany of the Spalding Club (1841), edited by a city advocate John Stuart.

No mention of the trial records was made in an inventory of Town Council files in 1851.

Perhaps these rare documents, a reminder of a terrible but important part of the city's history, might yet again see the light of day. Who knows?

Chapter Five

'The Highland Houdini'

'Stone walls do not a prison make,
Nor iron bars a cage'.
- Richard Lovelace.
(1618 - 1658).

Aberdonians hurry past the buildings with barely a hasty glance in the direction of its clock tower and golden weather cock. Rush hour traffic swirls within a few feet of the roughly-hewn walls of a squat tower that once served as a gloomy depository of the guilt and misery of bygone Bon-Accord.

'The Mids o' Mar', its red granite ashlers dulled with age, is the grimmest and yet most remarkable building in the city. The Tolbooth, former seat of civic business and jailhouse, has been a backdrop to life in the Castlegate since 1615.

Now it is almost tucked out of sight behind a Victorian facade of grey granite, ever since the present Town House replaced the old council chambers which stretched west of the Tolbooth tower. If it were not for the clock tower and spire, added at a later date, the keep tower would appear not to exist.

Soon citizens and visitors alike will have no excuse for being unaware of the Tolbooth's existence. The nail-studded doors and iron yetts which were erected to keep felons in, will one day be thrown open to visitors.

Even with its present embellishments the stone, barrel-vaulted dungeons chill the soul.

Harry Houdini might have experienced some difficulty in picking the huge locks and heavy chains. In the condemned cell criminals were shackled by the foot to the 'lang gade', or goad - a long, cylindrical-shaped iron bar bolted to the floor. Captives were allowed to move about their cell to the 'extent of their tether'.

As I negotiated the tortuous stairways and maze of cells I asked myself: 'How could anyone escape from this terrible place?'

Incredibly, prisoners did break free - many times.

To quote the 19th century Aberdeen author Dr Joseph Robertson: 'One feature which, in the eyes of its inmates, perhaps compensated for its filth, rigour, and gloom; it was marvellously unretentive'.

In 1638 Alexander Keith of Balmuir was smuggled out in a trunk, and his creditors sued the magistrates for the recovery of their claims. On a March night in 1675 Francis Irvine of Hilton and others jailed for debt caused 'afront and abuse' to the town when they smashed their way out of a cell in the upper storey and shinned down a rope to freedom. In 1690 James Gordon, a brother of the Laird of Arradoul, got his guards drunk and walked out of the front door. Their carelessness led to imprisonment, humiliation in the burgh stocks, and banishment for them and their families.

In February 1823 William MacLeod, Thomas Donaldson and Alexander Martin escaped while awaiting trial at the Circuit Court. They were recaptured and later hanged for their crimes.

But by far the prisoner whose escape fires the imagination was Peter Young, a famous caird - an itinerant tinker - who was bold and daring and slippery as an eel.

Tradition had it he escaped from every jail in Scotland and some swore there wasn't a prison built that would hold him.

Peter may have been unable to read nor write but he was clever with his hands. He fashioned 'chouries' - saw knives - to cut through his shackles and bars of his cell. He also had small neat hands, which enabled him to slip his handcuffs at will. And when all else failed Peter's natural cunning rarely let him down.

Peter's birthplace is a bit of a mystery. It is believed he was born at Mergie, northwest of Stonehaven, yet after escaping from the Tolbooth the proclamation said he was a native of Deeside. During an interrogation at Perth Jail, Peter said he came from Tillakeira, in the parish of Tough.

Peter was the son of James or Alexander Young - 'Caird Young' - and Ann Graham, whose brother was the 'king' of the Scottish gypsies. Charles Graham, nicknamed 'Gle'ed' because of a squint-eye, came from Lochgelly in Fife. He had succeeded the famous John Gun, a henchman of Rob Roy MacGregor. 'Caird' Young and Ann Graham had three sons - Robert, Peter and John, all of whom came to a sticky end.

Peter and his brothers were led into crime at an early age. As a wee boy Peter 'fished' for poultry with the aid of strong thread, a crooked pin and bread crumbs as bait.

His first venture - stealing from a farmer's house at Tough - failed, and he was soundly thrashed. After the Young brothers, Robert and Peter, gave a recruiting sergeant the slip, they moved their operations to the Cabrach. They fared little better. After another robbery they were arrested and sent to the Tolbooth in Aberdeen, where their height and build caught the eye of an army captain engaged in raising a company.

The officer decided jail was the best place for his new recruits until he was ready to march. But Peter hit on a novel idea. They concocted a paste and smeared it on their legs to give 'the appearance of being scorbutic', and were whisked off to the Infirmary in Woolmanhill. Despite a guard outside their door the brothers managed to leap from a second-storey window and get clean away. Back at the Tolbooth jailers found the fake paste and a large hole the Youngs had made at the back of the chimney in their cell.

Peter parted company from Robert, and crossed into England. He joined forces with another criminal and together they plundered a rich man's house near York, and got away with silver plate.

Before he returned to his native Scotland at the age of 18, Peter would pack a host of adventure (including fighting for both sides in the American War of Independence) into his short life.

He sailed from England in a privateer which was captured by an American frigate soon after leaving the English Channel. Peter and the rest of the crew were taken back to Boston, where he enlisted in Washington's Light Horse. He stayed for about a year, then deserted, taking with him a horse, arms and a uniform belonging to an officer. Peter reached British lines, and joined Colonel Tarleton's legion.

As the war neared its climax Peter again fell into American hands. He was not recognised as a deserter and was sent to Boston, where he was confined with other British prisoners. By fashioning saws from knives, he hacked through the bars of his cell and led fellow prisoners to freedom.

The escaped prisoners-of-war managed to board a small brigantine, deserted and riding at anchor in a creek, and weigh anchor. Luckily for the land-lubbers they met up with a British frigate. The captured brigantine was sailed to Halifax in Nova Scotia, where it was sold on behalf the ex-POWs, and the money divided amongst them.

Peter entered a line-of-battle ship and served as a seaman until the end of the war. An accidental fall from the yard-arm left him with a deep scar on the temple - a tell-tale mark which eventually led him to the gallows.

When the vessel reached England Peter deserted, taking with him a sum of money from the purser. He joined a privateer 'to cruise against the Dutch', but fell into their hands. Peter and his shipmates were held in Fort Lillo, but he managed to escape by scaling a high wall and swimming a moat. He swam a river and made his way to Ostende, where he joined a Scottish ship bound for the Firth of Forth.

On his return to his uncle, 'Gle'ed' Graham, in Lochgelly, he met and fell in love with Jean Wilson, daughter of James Wilson, who was hanged with his brother-in-law, John Brown, in Edinburgh in the autumn of 1773. Jean, who was about the same age as Peter, was adept as a pick-pocket thanks to the skills of her mother, Margaret Brown, and her aunt, Ann Brown, 'Gle'ed' Graham's wife.

Peter and Jean became husband and wife by mutual consent, without any legal or religious formalities, and then followed a criminal career throughout the North-east of Scotland. They specialised in picking pockets at local markets, where they posed as cattle dealers. They kept close together, and when one stole a purse or a pocket-book it was instantly handed to the other partner. Though Peter and his wife were arrested more than 20 times in markets in Aberdeenshire and Kincardinshire it was never possible to implicate them.

In time Peter built a reputation as a jail-breaker. At Charlestown of Aboyne he got away by jumping over the heads of spectators from the top, outer stair of the local clink. He walked away from Brechin Jail after cutting a bar from the window. Perth Jail held no fear for him after he was arrested on house-breaking charges. He escaped with members of his gang, including Ann Brown. The turnkey of Stonehaven's quayside tolbooth almost lost his job for allowing Peter to escape.

In May 1787, the gang, including Robert Young, met at a place called Greencairns of Balbegno. It was decided they would convene at Aberdeen on June 1. where large crowds were expected for the hanging of William Webster. (Ann Brown was caught picking pockets on the day and was ordered to be transported for seven years after being publicly whipped through the streets of Aberdeen).

Meanwhile Peter and Jean set out for Banffshire. They must have looked an incongruous couple. Both rode on a black horse, followed by a large brown dog, with a white neck, and an engraved brass collar. Peter sported a round slouched hat with a band fastened by an elegant Bristo'-set silver buckle. He wore riding boots. Their presence did not escape the local populace.

One night they raided John Reid's shop in Portsoy, riding off with a quantity of cottons, calicoes and other goods, to the value of £100. At Culsalmond, Jean left some of the stolen goods in the care of innocent country folk, pretending the packages were her spare clothes. Children would later describe Peter as 'a braw gentleman wi' a bonnie buckle in his hat'.

But the law was closing in on the gypsy rogues. After a series of incidents, during which the rest of the stolen goods were recovered, Peter and Jean were arrested and brought before the magistrate in Turriff. They pleaded ignorance but the dog inadvertently betrayed them. The couple were transferred to Banff Prison, from where they escaped in broad daylight! Peter dashed up a blind alley, hotly pursued by the jailer Daniel McDonald and outraged townsfolk. Jean got as far as Turriff on a stolen horse, but was soon recaptured. She was saddened her Peter had been 'ta'en afore he got awa the length o' his leg!'

Because of Peter's reputation for breaking out of jail, the Banff magistrates ordered that a round-the-clock guard be mounted outside his cell. They fettered him with heavy irons, as thick as a man's wrist, round his legs, with a large bar between them. Somehow Peter found the means to cut through his leg irons. He concealed his work by binding his legs with clouts, pretending the irons chaffed his legs. His plan was not to escape from the jail, but to make his break while being escorted back to Aberdeen where he was due to stand trial at the Autumn Circuit of 1787. But his plan back-fired and the couple were bound hard with ropes before being taken to Aberdeen.

They were both found guilty after trial. Jean Wilson pleaded that she was seven months pregnant, but a medical examination revealed she was only a short time gone. She was condemned to hang but because of her pregnancy the date of execution was put off until August 9, 1788.

Peter was sentenced to hang on the 16th of November.

Fate smiled kindly on Peter Young and his fellow prisoners in the Aberdeen Tolbooth.

For the jailer in charge, Andrew Gray, proved incompetent and would later be accused of being 'guilty of great negligence and inattention to the duties of his office'. Gray had allowed street pedlars to enter the jail to sell ale, beer and spirits to the prisoners. He entrusted the keys of the prison, day and night, to a poor servant, who, in turn, allowed anyone off the street to peer at condemned criminals, so long as they had a few coppers to spare.

Peter's friends managed to smuggle saw-knives to him but a search revealed nine such tools hidden up the chimney of his cell. Peter seemed resigned to his fate and requested clergymen to attend to his spiritual needs. One evening as Gray examined the bars of his windows, Peter said: 'Mr Gray, you need not look at the windows, for I assure you I will never go out of the prison till I go by the door.' Gray understood this to refer to Peter going out to the scaffold. The prisoner, it seemed, had other ideas.

Because he was illiterate Peter induced Gray to allow some of his fellow prisoners to read the Bible to him. Paddy Burns, James Memis and John Munro took turns to read to Peter behind a locked door. He in turn initiated them into the mysteries of picking locks and cutting iron bars. After they had cut through a window stanchion they filled the rent with grease and camouflaged it with iron rust.

And so Peter and six accomplices decided to escape from 'The Mids o' Mar on the night of October 24th.

After they had broken out of their cells in the upper portion of the Tolbooth they planned to release Jean Wilson and Ann Brown, the latter waiting to be transported overseas after her arrest at William Webster's execution. They were lodged in a cell below. They were unwittingly aided in the escape by the inner turnkey, who had made a slip-shod job of securing the locks and bolts of their cells.

Silent as wraiths, the prisoners picked locks, slid back bolts and forced their way through a strong iron door and equally strong oak door, not to mention cell doors and an iron yett. This they accomplished by brute force and cunning, using everything from an old nail to a heated iron spike.

After they had unlocked the door of the cell holding the two women the prison-breakers slipped away one-by-one into the street on their bare feet. Behind the jail the guard was being changed. It was three o'clock in the morning of October the 25th.

The gang headed westwards. It consisted of Peter Young, his wife Jean Wilson, her aunt Ann Brown, John Paul under sentence of death for sheep-stealing, Paddy Burns, William Bartlet, a soldier who had killed a man in a fight, Patrick Anderson, a boy facing transportation, John Memis, thief and housebreaker, and John Munro, a noted thief who would later be hanged in Aberdeen. (Munro, on being pressed by a clergyman to confess or go to hell, replied there were 'many coot shentlemens there'.)

Peter, always the humanitarian, carried Memis, who was old and infirm, for several miles on his back.

The escape was discovered at six in the morning. The magistrates were livid. The jailer Gray, who it seems had been tipped off by mealsellers of the prisoners' attempts to cut through the window bars, was soon stripped of his post.

Peter and his comrades then made their escape south by Den of Durris. It is possible they 'lurked' for a time in Red Beard's Cave on the slopes of Craigbeg, an area Peter would have known well if he was born at Mergie. The cave, which no longer exists, was a favourite hiding place for 'cairds'. Red Beard's Well still bubbles forth on the east side of the Cryne Corse path on Craigbeg.

Eventually the party was spotted descending the hills north of Laurencekirk. Peter was heading for Mill of Kincardine, the home of a coarse character, James Strachan, who befriended criminals. On a previous visit, Peter and his brother Robert had concocted a scheme to rob the home of Sir Alexander Ramsay of Fasque.

Sir Edward Bannerman of Phesdo House led a party of policemen and servants to Mill of Kincardine. As they surrounded the house Peter Young escaped by a back window. Anderson, too, got away, but the other escapees, including the two women, were recaptured.

It appears Sir Edward was on the point of shooting Peter when he tripped and fell, and the famous caird, who hated violence, showed a clean pair of heels.

A reward of 20 guineas was offered by Aberdeen magistrates for Peter's recapture while a 'handsome reward' was offered for the arrest of Anderson.

The proclamation gives us a detailed description of Peter: 'A stout young man, pockpitted, aged about twenty-two, with a remarkably sharp eye; about five feet ten inches high, thin made, has an arch-sneering look; is a native of Deeside, in the county of

Aberdeen, the language of which he speaks.' Peter, ever the sharp dresser, was wearing a 'tartan short jacket of large squares or lozens, trousers of the same stuff, and a bonnet, so that he is rather a remarkable figure.' Indeed, he was!

The fugitive Peter wandered the hills of Angus and would later scotch a report that he had been spotted in Aberdeen's Hardgate dressed as a woman!

In December 1787 he strode the streets of Perth where the previous year he had broken out of the local jailhouse. He and some associates entered the Church of Aberdagie, stripped the pulpit of its green velvet cloth, and Lord Kinnoul's loft of the purple velvet chair covers. They also took the pewter baptism basin, believing it to be silver.

The debonair rogue made himself a handsome jacket of the pulpit cloth, which he trimmed with fringes, and a vest from the chair covers. It is said he created a sensation when he appeared in his strange garb at the local market. But Peter was a superstitious fellow and the theft from the kirk would prey on his mind.

Peter fell in with his uncle, 'Gle'ed' Graham, and together they headed for Aberdeen. In their heads they had a scheme to rescue their wives. But they could not resist carrying out two burglaries in the Arbroath area, which resulted in their arrest. Peter gave a fictitious name but a gentleman recognised him by the scar on his temple.

Peter was clapped in the stocks in Arbroath prison and the Aberdeen magistrates notified. An officer was dispatched from Aberdeen to identify the elusive prisoner. His journey was wasted. By the time he arrived in Arbroath Peter and his uncle had fled. During the night they had been moved to a cell with a roaring fire and by morning both men had gone.

They refused to be beaten by the snowdrifts which covered the countryside, and got as far as the Bridge of Dun when the Sheriff's men rode upon them.

Graham was quickly overpowered, but Peter, although handicapped by his handcuffs, bolted for cover in the woods of Dunsmills. A little dog accompanying the pursuers sniffed out Peter as he hid in a ditch under a wreath of snow. A careless jailer was blamed for the double escape, but Peter, on his recapture, claimed he had bribed the man 50 shillings to unlock the cell door.

On New Year's Day 1788 a huge crowd milled around the

Tolbooth in Aberdeen to see the return of Peter Young. To prevent another escape attempt the window stanchions had been renewed, the flagstones in the cells had been taken up and re-laid, and a thorough search made for 'chouries'.

He was strip-searched and put in a cell on his own, and orders given that no one was allowed to see him but the jailer. Eleven days later Paddy Burns and Anderson were returned to the Tolbooth.

Peter's cell was damp, airless and had no heating.

Two local doctors, George Skene and Alexander Bannerman, complained about the conditions to the magistrates. They said the prisoner's health was in danger and recommended he be moved to a cell with fresh air and a fireplace. This was duly done.

The enterprising Peter made a final bid to escape from Aberdeen. He got his hands on six shoemakers' paring knives, fashioned into files, which were smuggled into the jail in a jug of broth brought by a woman.

Before he could free himself a macer arrived from Edinburgh on January 18th, with orders to take him back to the capital. As he descended the Tolbooth stairs his wife called out to him: 'Oh, Peter, Peter, you shou'd hae bidden out o' their grips when you was out o' their grips—I'll never see you again'!

On the road Peter expressed a wish to lodge at Perth jail. He told his escort, 'he had, or would get something there which would be of use to him'. Perhaps he had some of his ubiquitous 'chouries' hidden away?

On arriving at 'The Heart of Midlothian' - the Edinburgh Tolbooth - Peter was put on the 'lang gade'.

Within and hour the inner turnkey caught his very important prisoner busily cutting through a leg iron with a saw-knife. A body search revealed two additional knives concealed in the inner sole of his shoe.

On Monday, March 3, the celebrated caird stood at the bar of the High Court of Justiciary. He was not in the least bit overawed by the majesty of the law. When the Lord Justice Clerk asked if he had anything to say why execution of his former sentence of death, imposed in Aberdeen in 1787, should not be carried out, Peter replied: 'I am not the man'.

Peter's counsel, Charles Hope, later to become a leading Scottish judge, vigorously pleaded Peter's case - that, as the prisoner had denied his identity, it was his right as a British subject to have the question tried by a jury, as it was a question of fact, and not a point of law. That set the venerable Law Lords scratching their wigs. The case was adjourned until the 14th when the Lordships gave their judgment. It was decided no jury was required.

The next day William Stewart, who had been a macer at the Autumn Circuit in Aberdeen in 1787, and Alexander Guthrie, the Circuit Clerk, swore to the prisoner's identity, referring in particular to the scar on his temple.

Peter Young was sentenced to die on the second day of April. Now fully aware of their prisoner's 'Houdini-like' abilities, a special cage was built for him in the Tolbooth.

His lawyers were able to gain a brief respite and the execution date was postponed until Wednesday, 2 July, 1788.

Six days before the hanging Peter dictated a letter to his wife. Part of the letter read:

'I hope in God you will get liberty: and if you do, I hope you will take care and keep it. When you are brought to bed, if you have a son, I desire you will call him after me: and if you get liberty, and the child and you are spared together, I hope you will do your endeavour to bring it up in an honest way... My dear, what could a man do more than lay down his life to save his wife's? For in coming to save yours I lost my own.'

He enclosed a lock of his hair. No doubt Peter held out hope of a pardon or a chance to escape, but on June 25 'Aberdeen Journal' readers learned that an Aberdeen minister, Reverend Moodie, had informed the prisoner there was no prospect of a reprieve. Peter was a dead man. Mr Moodie was at his side when he faced the hangman with firmness and great courage on the scaffold at the west end of the Edinburgh Tolbooth. His executioner was most likely John High, nicknamed Jock Heich, who held office from 1784 to 1817. Aberdeen's hangman Johnny Milne stole bees before getting the job as executioner. Jock Heich had stolen poultry.

On the day he died Peter's wife gave birth to a daughter in Aberdeen Tolbooth. Peter was 24 years old.

The well-known Aberdeen minister Dr. James Kidd is said to have taken a 'friendly and helpful' interest in Peter Young. Peter gave the minister an exquisite carving as a keepsake. To his unborn child his only legacy, he said, was the 102nd Psalm in the long metre and an earnest prayer the youngster would 'believe in the Lord and lead a good life instead of the wicked one his father had followed'.

Kidd's biographer claimed Peter's offspring was a boy, although the daughter born to Jean was said to have been their only child. Kidd took the boy under his fatherly wing and gave him an education before he joined the army.

When the wretched vaults of the Tolbooth became dilapidated and too small to hold prisoners it was decided to build a new jail in Aberdeen. The East Prison sprung up directly behind the Tolbooth in 1829, and had 60 cells for male prisoners only. The East Prison served Aberdeen and the county for the next 60 years and more.

It was closed in June 1891 when the new prison opened at the Craiglug on the Torry bank of the Dee. On June 9, 43 prisoners were transferred from Lodge Walk to Craiginches by horse-drawn buses.

Plans were already afoot for new police headquarters in Lodge Walk but there was some debate as to whether the East Prison should be reconstructed or demolished. The latter course was chosen and a spanking new Aberdeen City Police HQ building, complete with electric light, gymnasium and glass-enclosed bridge to the adjoining Sheriff Courthouse, was opened in October, 1895.

So 'The Mids o' Mar', which stands on the foundations of a 14th century prison, which in its turn replaced an earlier Tolbooth of greater antiquity in Virginia Street, is to get a new lease of life.

The modern refurbishments include lighting and a lift connecting the Town House with the old condemned cell.

Peter Young would have liked that!

Chapter Six

Riotous Behaviour

The Plainstones ran red with blood when King George the Third's birthday celebrations turned into a massacre of the innocents.

The Ross and Cromarty Rangers, described as an 'ill-behaved corps' of Highlanders and Irishmen, turned their muskets on the public when horseplay got out of hand.

Friday, June 4, 1802, began brightly and optimistically enough with young tradesman marching through Aberdeen with colours flying and drums beating. Also at noon the garrison troops fired three volleys in the air in the barrack square.

The celebrations went on in Castle Street until after dark, as Provost James Hadden and magistrates entertained prominent citizens and officers of the Ross and Cromarty Rangers in the Town Hall, directly opposite the 'Plainstaines', a raised platform of smooth granite slabs, extending from the Exchange coffee house to the Market Cross, where merchants, addicted to strolling together to discuss business, were known as peripatetics.

When the officers appeared from the Town Hall they were rather the worse of liquor and the crowd of spectators, who had been good humouredly bating the Rangers mounting guard at the guardhouse, turned their attention to the new arrivals.

Mud, squibs, garbage - even a dead cat or two - were thrown at the officers and their men. Insults were traded and Captain Felix Macdonogh drew his sword but made light of the incident by doffing his hat and joining in the high spirits and cheers of the spectators.

The Town Clerk was summoned but he showed little sympathy, telling the mud-spattered captain that the crowd 'had done nothing to him but what they did to every well-dressed person on similar occasions'. Two Town Sergeants escorted the officer across the street.

Colonel Mackenzie, who was hopelessly drunk, almost tumbled down the stairs of the Town Hall, to the delight of the spectators.

46

Mackenzie, who fell more than once as he staggered across the street, gave orders to call out the regiment. With the insults of the crowd ringing in his ears the brave Colonel was led off to his quarters in the barracks where he did not stir that night.

Macdonogh, sensing revenge, took command of the armed troops and gave orders to fire. A hail of lead whistled across the street drilling holes in property - and people.

John Ross, a private in the local rifle corps, was shot in the head as he stood on the Plainstones, and died instantly. Thomas Milne, a mason, and two boys, John Moir and William Gibb, a barber's apprentice, died of their wounds the following day. At least 10 persons were wounded.

The massacre did not quell the rioting troops and it took a courageous man - Provost James Hadden - to force the troops to return to the barracks. At one stage he showed an obstinate Sergeant Andrew Mackay, his chain of office, and dealing the man a sharp blow shouted: 'Will you obey that!'

A guard of armed citizens took to the streets to preserve law and order while Provost Hadden confronted a drunken Colonel Mackenzie in the barracks and charged him with murder. The Colonel, Captain Macdonogh, and six other soldiers were arrested.

At midnight, four days later, the disgraced regiment, each man on his stocking soles, marched silently out of Aberdeen and headed north, one column taking the road to Oldmeldrum and the other to Ellon. The prisoners were locked up in the Tolbooth until June 17 when they were shipped to Edinburgh in the cutter Royal Charlotte to await trial.

In January 1803 Colonel Mackenzie, Captain Macdonogh and Sergeants Andrew Mackay and Alex Sutherland, went on trial at the High Court of Justiciary in Edinburgh, charged with the murder of Rifleman Ross. They all pleaded not guilty.

The jury at the end of the protracted trial found the officers not guilty and the charge against the NCOs not proven. Another accused, Ensign Lanigan, who had absconded before the trial, was outlawed.

The Plainstones Massacre apart, the worst ever disturbance in Aberdeen began with an inquisitive dog digging in the ground behind Dr Andrew Moir's new anatomical theatre in Hospital Row.

The population was highly suspicious of the gloomy building with its false church-looking windows, overlooking St Andrew Street.

47

They were haunted by the revelations of Burke and Hare, the 'Wolves of the West Port', who traded in dead flesh and murdered 16 persons, selling their corpses to the Edinburgh anatomist, Dr Knox.

At the beginning of December 1831, only a few weeks after Dr Moir delivered his first lecture - the 'Aberdeen Journal' reported the execution and confessions of the 'London Burkers', Bishop and Williams, and the alleged attempt to 'burke' a boy by two, well-dressed and rather young men in John Street, yards from the new anatomical theatre. No violence had been involved. The men had simply asked the boy to run an errand but he took fright and fled. The activities of local body-snatchers were still fresh in the memory and kirkyards were still guarded by the bereaved and watchmen.

So it began with a dog, that Monday, the 19th, tearing at something in the ground. A knot of urchins investigated and were joined by some tannery workers. A crowd of spectators grew and there was a cry of horror when the tanners unearthed some fragments of a human body, probably dumped by a careless porter employed by Dr Moir.

This grisly find sparked off the 'Burkin' Hoose Riot'. It did not end until the building was razed to the ground by fire and sheer muscle power. It was a miracle no lives were lost.

Dr Moir - known as 'Clever, dirty Andrew Moir' - because of his habit of joining students on their nocturnal body-snatching raids was preparing for an afternoon lecture when the mob swarmed into the building.

He and his students were brutally assaulted, and were lucky to escape, after first barricading themselves in a different part of the building. The rioters burst into the dissecting room and found three corpses. The remains were carried on makeshift stretchers to Drum's Aisle in the Mither Kirk.

Dr Moir evaded capture although pursued through the streets by the mob. Bloodthirsty cries of 'Burn the hoose, down wi' the Burkin' shop' rent the night air as the mob turned their fury on the empty 'Burkin' Hoose'.

Using the mason's timber, shavings, fir and tar barrel staves for fuel, the rioters set the building ablaze. Then they began to pound the masonry with planks and anything they could lay their hands on.

Provost Hadden was again in office that year and had a hand

in quelling the rioters. The 79th Regiment (Cameron Highlanders) stood guard on the other side of the wall of Gordon's Hospital. Perhaps the Provost feared another Plainstones Massacre. But the Camerons were made of sterner stuff. The fire brigade was helpless. Its way was blocked by the mob. Up to 12,000 people watched the destruction of the anatomical theatre, and few had any sympathy for Dr Moir. He later accused the 'Aberdeen Journal' of 'befriending incendiarists'.

At the circuit Court in April 1832 three men faced charges of mobbing, rioting, wilful fire-raising and assault.

They were flesher Alexander Murray, of West North Street, Aberdeen; blacksmith George Sharpe, of Schoolhill, and Alexander Allan, a private in the Fusilier Guards. The indictment alleged they were 'part of a mob of disorderly and evil disposed persons'.

The Advocate-Depute, admitting it was a peculiar case, accepted a modified plea of mobbing and rioting and to depart from the capital charge of wilful fire-raising. It appeared, he said, to have been carelessness on the part of the doctors which led to the formidable riot. The charges of assault on Dr Moir and a medical student, James Polson, who was saved from severe injury through the timely arrival of a policeman, were dropped.

The accused were all of good character and had not been the ringleaders. Sharpe told the court he had 'merely gone to the spot to examine among the human remains lying there, whether he could discover the body of his grandmother, who had been interred a few weeks previously'.

Lord Moncrieff said the charges against them went to the violation of all law and decency. If they had been incited by the foolish delusion that the very respectable gentlemen who possessed the building, or any other engaged in the pursuit, was capable of wilful murder for the purpose of science, 'this was a feeling unworthy of every well educated and well disposed Scotsman'. They were each jailed for one year.

Dr Moir became the target of bullies and ruffians. His house in the Guestrow was pelted with rotten vegetables and dead poultry, and a lantern was torn down and kicked football-fashion along the street by youths.

He and his financial backers claimed damages from the Town Council, asserting, not enough had been done to save the anatomical theatre, and they eventually received £235 compensation.

Dr Moir did continue to lecture in the city, and was eventually appointed in 1839 lecturer in anatomy at a medical school founded by King's College in a house in Kingsland Place, Old Aberdeen. In that same year he married an old sweetheart, Agnes Fraser, on her return from Canada.

Tragedy struck while he was making up for lost ground in his career and his wife was expecting their second child. Dr Moir died on February 6, 1844, at the age of 38, after taking ill with typhoid fever.

He is buried in St Nicholas Churchyard. His table tombstone stands near the Schoolhill gate, and is very much like the one he hid under the night his world went up in flames.

Riotous behaviour was not confined to the hoi polloi. A 'riot' broke out during the installation of a new rector at Aberdeen University on Saturday, 16 March 1861. The Right Hon. Edward Francis Maitland, Solicitor General for Scotland (later Lord Barcaple) was an unpopular choice, and when the academics entered Marischal College hall for the ceremony all hell broke loose. The new rector was struck by a missile, as angry students smashed benches and seats and hurled them at the VIPs. The rector abandoned his address and the police were called. Principal Campbell told the unruly students: 'Your prospects in life are ruined by the proceedings of today; some of you not only make use of the expressions of opinion, but use dangerous missiles'.

This steep flight of stairs at Castlehill, Aberdeen, roughly marks the place where Hangman's Brae stood.

Gallow Hill in Aberdeen's Errol Street. Until 1776 criminals were executed and exhibited in chains at this spot.

Death Machine. Artist's impression of the Edinburgh decapitating machine, 'The Maiden'. There was a similar one in Aberdeen. (From Grant's 'Old and New Edinburgh').

Aberdeen executioner Johnny Milne chooses a fish - the Hangman's perk - in Seaton's 'View of Castle Street, 1806'. The town drummer was a far more popular figure. (Author's Collection).

Chapter Seven

'Leud Leivars Pyikers and Harlottis'

Aberdeen's first House of Correction has long vanished - but its name lives on in a street of undistinguished buildings that winds its way past the east wall of St Nicholas Churchyard.

The 'correction hous' was a working house for the manufacture of 'broad cloths, kerseys, broad and other coarse clothes'. It was run as a private enterprise and under the management of the Town Council.

It was built by two Englishmen, brothers Robert and Nicholas Beastoun, under a patent obtained from Charles the First in 1636.

The Aberdeen House of Correction was one of the first of its kind in Scotland. The driving force was Provost Alexander Jaffray, who formed a joint-stock company because the cost of building the place was too expensive for the burgh.

The magistrates contributed 2,000 merks towards the enterprise and reserved the right to send there 'all vagabonds, strong and sturdie beggars, idle and maisterless personyes, strong in bodie and habill to work, servants disobedient to maistris, children disobedient to parentis, leud leivars, pyikers, common scolds and incorrigible harlottis not amending to the discipline of the kirk'.

Life was tough for the inmates and it is on record how a frail woman was publicly whipped once a week while serving her time.

But some prisoners survived the regime - no matter their age. In August 1835 a thief, Janet Ross, was sent to the Bridewell for nine months. At the age of 90! The mystery was how a habitual law-breaker, had escaped transportation - even the gallows.

The House of Correction figured in 'The Trubles'. After the Battle of Justice Mills in September 1644 Montrose's Irish mercenaries plundered and raped the town, carrying off cloth and kersey worth £1,860 Scots, after freeing inmates from the Correction House and the Tolbooth.

More than 100 men from all walks of Aberdeen life were killed and when Montrose's men returned the following year he gave his word that his 'Wild Geese' would not be allowed within eight miles of the town. Even so Montrose again had his eyes on the Correction House factory for in January 1645 he demanded English cloth for making suits for himself and brother officers, as well as stockings, 'otherwayes they would not be able to save the booths of the town unplunderit altogidder'.

The House of Correction enterprise failed and the concern was discontinued in 1711 and the property sold.

Aberdeen's second correction house, the Bridewell, took its name, as similar establishments did, from a palace built by King John in the London parish of St Bride. By the reign of Edward VI it maintained the poor of London and later became a house of correction.

The Aberdeen Bridewell was completed in 1809, and stood at the opposite end of the burgh, in Rose Street, which was then a cul-de-sac.

Architect James Burns designed a castellated-style five-floored building, with hospital, workroom and cells for both sexes. There was a separate block with kitchens, chapel, meeting rooms and apartments for the resident surgeon and governor.

The Bridewell gardens and exercise yards were surrounded with a 14ft high wall, the northern boundary of which touched Henry Street, now Skene Street, with the main gate and guardhouse facing Union Street.

The cost of the building - including 'steaming apparatus, bedding, clothing and other furnishings' - was about £10,000.

The upkeep of the Bridewell was shared between town and county, although the greater proportion of prisoners came from the town. 'The Black Kalendar of Aberdeen' insisted: 'Almost all our great Aberdeen criminals have come from the country'. The largest number of prisoners confined in the Bridewell at one time was 48 - 31 males and 17 females, with 34 from the town and 14 from the country.

It wasn't a home from home and in June 1831 an escape bid was foiled. The prisoner Robert Gallie, junior, had been sent to the Bridewell for a year. Less than two months later the young weaver made his break for freedom. He cut a hole in the door of his cell, which was on the third floor.

By forcing the lock of another door, raising flagstones and ripping out a ventilator he managed to reach the first floor. But the prison break failed when Gallie was confronted by a turnkey, John Barnett. There was a furious struggle which resulted in the governor, Mr W.C. Chalmers, being hurt.

The Bridewell, sometimes known as the Town and County Jail, underwent a final name change in 1842.

It became the 'West Prison'. The East Prison in Lodge Walk had grown in size and was about to take on the role as the town's chief prison.

The gates of Bridewell closed for all time in 1868.

Two years later the jail was no more. A bare memory caught in sketches and faded photographs. It disappeared along with the horse-drawn 'Rose Street omnibus' which transported prisoners.

The gap was filled for a brief time by a pleasure garden. The Aberdeen advocate Lachlan Mackinnon attended the inaugural fete in his schooldays. Along with other spectators he took his life into his hands to watch a none-too-expert athlete demonstrate a new technique for throwing the hammer. They also thrilled at the antics of 'The Man Fish' in a water-filled tank.

Chapter Eight

Vinter From the Other World

Alexander Milne's map of Aberdeen in 1789 pinpoints the scene of the city's greatest scandal.

'The Old Barn where kidnapped boys were kept', stood on the south-east corner of Renny's Wynd, now Rennie's Wynd, a nondescript street at the back of the Tivoli.

Between 1740 and 1746 alone, 600 youngsters of both sexes and ranging from the age of six upwards were seized and shipped to North America where they were sold as slaves.

The vile trade - called 'listing' to give it an air of respectable business - was carried out in Aberdeen, and other Scottish towns, from an earlier date.

Aberdeen's kidnapping industry was not run by a gang of desperadoes but by a group of well-doing and respected citizens, headed by William Fordyce of Auquhorties, a merchant, baillie and treasurer of the burgh in 1736. His partners in crime included his father-in-law, Walter Cochran, the town clerk depute, and Alexander Mitchell of Colpna, now Orrok.

Justice caught up with them in June 1758, when Peter Williamson arrived in the Castlegate dressed as an American Indian and armed to the teeth. And he was definitely not smoking a 'peace pipe'.

Peter, who was born in Hirnlay, near Aboyne, in 1730, was snatched during a visit to his aunt in Aberdeen in January 1743. The 'rough, ragged, humble-headed, long, stowie, clever boy' was enticed aboard the ship, Kenilworth, while playing on the quayside.

The man who 'sold' Peter in Aberdeen was paid one shilling and sixpence.

During the month the ship lay in port Peter and his fellow travellers were kept hidden below decks. Elsewhere children and youths were rounded up like cattle and sold into slavery, even by their own families to stave off hunger. In Aberdeen they were imprisoned in the old barn, or locked up in the House of Correction or Tolbooth.

They passed the time in confinement playing cards, eating and drinking. A bagpiper was hired to entertain or deaden the noise of crying by the very young. Their future was bleak for many committed suicide because of their treatment by the slave-masters.

Peter survived a stormy, 11-week crossing of the Atlantic, and a midnight shipwreck off Cape May. The captain and crew abandoned the Palatines (as the Aberdeen youngsters sold into slavery were called) but returned for the human cargo when the storm abated. Peter was landed at Philadelphia where he was sold for seven years for a price of £16 to Scotsman Hugh Wilson, who had in his youth been kidnapped in Perth.

Wilson proved a 'humane, worthy, honest man' and having no family of his own he sent his charge to school for five winters. On his death, when Peter was 17, Wilson left him £150 currency, his best horse, saddle and his entire wardrobe.

The future looked rosy for young Peter.

He wooed and married a planter's daughter and his father-in-law gifted him 200 acres of land on the Pennsylvanian border, near the forks of the River Delaware, in Berks county. But Peter's good fortune ended when Indians, in the pay of the French, raided the territory.

On the night of October 2, 1754, while his wife was visiting relatives, a war party attacked their house. Peter was forced to surrender. Surprisingly, in light of the atrocities he later witnessed, the Indians made him their prisoner. The raiders torched the house and barn, destroying crops, cattle and horses. Peter was carried off, and although spared, he was tortured for the amusement of his captors.

During the three months he was held captive Peter studied their dress, customs and barbaric method of waging war on the helpless settlers and their families. Peter managed to escape but on his homecoming found that his wife had died soon after his capture.

Peter gave a graphic account of his ordeal to the State Assembly, turned his back on the soil and enlisted in a regiment under the command of General Shirley, Governor of New England, in the war against the French.

Peter's life of adventure resembled a novel by James Fenimore Cooper. He was taken prisoner by Montcalm's forces at the fall of Fort Oswego in August 1756. The victors pillaged the fort and slaughtered the wounded, but Peter suffered only a hand wound. He was repatriated by the French. On landing at Plymouth he was discharged from the army because of his wound, and received a gratuity of six shillings.

Short of money by the time he reached York he persuaded local businessmen to sponsor the publication of his memoirs, grandly entitled, 'French and Indian Cruelty exemplified in the Life and various Vicissitudes of Fortune of Peter Williamson, who was carried off from Aberdeen, in his Infancy, and sold as a slave in Pennsylvania'. It sold 1,750 copies in York and Newcastle and made Peter a profit of £30. More than 30 editions of the book have been published since.

Peter had a keen eye for publicity. Whenever he sold his book he would dress up in Indian costume and warpaint, and brandish a tomahawk and a musket.

For good measure he would break into a war dance and release bloodcurdling whoops.

He proved a sensation when he arrived in Aberdeen in search of his long lost relatives - and further sales of his book.

In his memoirs Peter told how worthy merchants of Aberdeen had been involved in the 'villainous and execrable practice' of kidnapping. He would later write of the 'very barbarous usage and ill treatment' he received in the burgh, 'occasioned by complaining against the illegal practice'.

Outraged by his revelations the magistrates accused Peter of publishing 'a scurrilous and infamous libel on the Corporation of the City of Aberdeen, and whole members thereof'. He was convicted and tossed in jail until he signed a statement denying the truth of the accusations. The hangman tore the offending pages from Peter's book and publicly burned them at the Market Cross. (On other occasions the hangman did the same to an offending copy of the 'Aberdeen Journal', and to Statio Ross's showbox because he had insulted an army officer). Peter reluctantly signed the document, and, after being fined 10 shillings, was banished from the town.

But Peter Williamson, Indian fighter and great survivor, had a score to settle. Lawyers in Edinburgh took up his case against the Aberdeen magistrates and in 1762 the Court of Sessions awarded him £100 damages plus £80 expenses, 'for which the lords declared the defenders to be personally liable, and that the same shall be no burden upon the town of Aberdeen'.

The wily magistrates managed to evade the decree of court by paying the damages and costs from the Common Good Fund, which has its origins in the gift of the Stocket Forest to Aberdeen by King Robert the Bruce.

But Peter was not finished with his kidnappers, at least those who were still alive. Unable to raise a criminal prosecution, Williamson's lawyers raised an action for damages against Fordyce and the surviving 'kidnappers'.

The 'kidnappers' managed to persuade Peter's lawyers that the case should go to arbitration by the Sheriff-Substitute in Aberdeen, James Forbes of Shields. Forbes retired to Archibald Campbell's howff, where he drank 'helter-skelter' (thanks to the 'kidnappers') quantities of spirits, white wine and hot punch.

A bleary-eyed Sheriff Forbes ruled in favour of the 'kidnappers', who had the verdict read out at the Plainstones. But the Court of Session once again stepped in and in February 1768 Peter won his case, and was awarded £200 damages and £100 expenses against Fordyce and others.

A triumphant Peter Williamson settled in Edinburgh, where he opened a printer's shop at the head of Forrester's Wynd, off the Lawnmarket, in 1772. He launched 'The Scots Spy', a weekly publication, in 1776.

At a new tavern and printing shop in the Luckenbooths, above which hung a sign proclaiming: 'Peter Williamson, Vinter from the other World' (reference to his globe-trotting activities), he published his highly successful street directory of Edinburgh. Magistrates would gather in the tavern to partake of the 'deid-chack' - a dinner at the expense of the city - after having attended a hanging. Lord Provost Creech abandoned the practice.

The famous Scottish poet Robert Fergusson referred to Peter's tavern in his poem, The Rising of the Session:-

'This vacance is a heavy doom
On Indian Peter's coffee-room,
For a' his china pigs are toom;
Nor do we see
In wine the soukar biskets soom
As light's a flee'.

Peter's other accomplishments ranged from the invention of a reaping machine to the establishment of the capital's first penny

59

post, for which he received a handsome compensation from a grateful Government.

Peter remarried. His wife and daughter were nimble-fingered, making everything from silk gloves to shrouds!

On that grave note it should be said Peter, one of the most colourful characters to set foot in Aberdeen, died on January 19, 1799, in his 69th year.

Chapter Nine

'Poor Ritchie'

In the summer of 1818 small knots of folk congregated at the Tolbooth in Aberdeen to pick up folded bits of paper that occasionally floated down on their heads from the barred window of a cell.

The 'billets' were allegedly penned by James Ritchie, 'whose youthful and comely' appearance had captured the imagination of the burgh, if not the whole of North-east Scotland. In some quarters it was whispered he was revered as a saint, rather than a criminal about to hang at the age of only 17.

Ritchie's crime was the theft of 30 sheep from the parks at Gordon Castle, Fochabers, the home of Alexander, 4th Duke of Gordon, whose beautiful wife it was said helped raise the Gordon Highlanders by offering each new recruit a shilling and a kiss. It was believed the boy had been the 'dupe of more adroit thieves'.

Sheep-stealers and horse-thieves could expect little mercy in those days and the general feeling was that an example was being made of Ritchie.

Some accused of the crime of sheep-stealing would rather take their own life than face the gallows.

A Strathbogie butcher William Still was being brought to Aberdeen for trial in 1751 when, according to the grim humour of the 'Aberdeen Journal', 'in order to save the trouble of a long journey, and the tedious process of a long trial, he hanged himself in his garters'.

In January 1818, the same month Ritchie was arrested, James Grant was apprehended in Montrose where he sold sheep he had rustled at Bridge of Dye. Grant was being escorted into Aberdeen across the Bridge of Dee when he hurled himself over the parapet to be 'dashed to pieces' 25 feet below.

The 'Aberdeen Chronicle' remarked of Grant's death: 'He made an example of himself as impressive as if he had suffered in our market place'. Cattle thieves were paraded in a bizarre fashion through the streets of Aberdeen.

The 'Aberdeen Journal' of January 9, 1753: 'On Saturday, Alexander Martin, tenant in Westertown of Huntly was brought to the city, and incarcerated in the tolbooth, by a warrant from the Sheriff, for stealing and slaughtering an ox, the property of William Anderson, in Cairntown of Cowburty. He was wrapped in the oxhide by way of a great-coat with the horns properly placed'.

In May 1751 William Macdonald and Elspet Grant, sheepstealers, were carried through the town in a cart, with two sheepskins on their necks, their hands bound behind their backs, and attended by the public hangman.

A wave of sympathy went out to Ritchie when his background was made public.

He had been born on April 19, 1801, at Gardenstown, on the ruggedly beautiful Banffshire coast. He was an orphan, his father having died when he was two, and his mother dying when he was 12.

At the age of 13 he worked as a gardener for a wealthy landlord, Mr Garden of Troup, but he ran away. According to a report at the time of his execution he followed a 'sinful and vicious course of life' in London, where he and a fellow servant appeared before a court on a charge of theft but he was acquitted.

As Ritchie had a clean sheet before the Gordon case strenuous efforts were made to gain him a respite. People from all walks of life, university professors, the clergy and members of the business community got up petitions.

The Duke of Gordon was approached but in the beginning he appeared to turn a deaf ear to pleas to intercede.

Ritchie was due to keep his date with the hangman on Friday, the 5th of June.

During his time in the death cell Ritchie constantly had a minister of religion at his ear. It was reported that he 'listened with much earnestness to the exhortations' of these clergymen - five in all, Rev. Mr Thom the jail chaplain; the Rev. Dr Brown, Rev. Dr Ross, Mr, later Dr James Kidd and Mr Valentine Ward, of the Wesleyan Methodists.

Grave were the utterances made by poor James Ritchie. In the days before the fateful day his letters, admitting the folly of his ways, and urging people not to follow his footsteps in crime, showered down from his cell. That the local clergy - his 'dear instructors' - had a hand in these epistles there is no doubt.

Ritchie went to the gallows with a prayer on his lips. He made his appearance on the scaffold five minutes after the clocks of the burgh had struck two. As was the custom, he dressed in a shroud.

A contemporary report tells how Ritchie 'maintained a composure and firmness superior for his years, exciting the astonishment of the very numerous spectators, who witnessed the revolting spectacle'.

It was noted that his time behind bars had 'imparted an uncommon delicacy to his complexion. Ritchie bowed to the clergyman on the scaffold and 'died with but little struggle', at the hands of Johnny Milne o' Tillyskukie. The boy sheep-stealer was given no respite from his speech writers. A broadsheet headed 'Last Speech, confession and dying declaration' embroidered with illustrations of an hour glass, skull and crossbones, was sold in the streets soon after the hanging.

Ritchie is quoted thus: 'My first thought in particular is to think what a hardened mortal I have been to continue so long hardened in my sin, knowing the time was appointed that I should appear before the Judgement Seat'. And so on, and so on.

Even as Ritchie's corpse swung like a tassel on the rope Reverend Ward took the opportunity to deliver from the scaffold a discourse, mainly about breaking the Sabbath. Long before that happened a large section of the crowd, some in tears, had departed the sad scene.

In 1927, Louisa Innes Lumsden, said that one of her mother's earliest recollections was of the day of Ritchie's hanging and of a crowd of people, mostly women, passing the gate of Springhill House 'in great excitement' following the execution. 'There was great indignation of this execution and the cruelty of the law'.

However her mother's memory failed her. 'A man had been apprehended at the same time as the boy,' wrote Lumsden,' and the two were being taken to prison in a cart, when the man sprang out, jumped over the bridge across the Denburn in Union Street and was killed'. She was obviously referring to Grant's suicide leap at the Brig o' Dee.

A war of words followed Ritchie's tragic death.

The general feeling was that the elderly Duke of Gordon had not done enough to save the boy's neck.

It had been recalled that a cattle thief, William Souter, son of Lord Halkerston's ground officer, was saved from hanging in Aberdeen in July 1774 because of his age - 20. He was banished to the plantations for life.

But the Duke of Gordon did make a last minute effort to have Ritchie pardoned, but his appeal to the Home Secretary failed.

Notice of the Duke's unsuccessful plea for mercy was contained in a letter which arrived in Aberdeen from London the day after the hanging.

Lewis Smith, the Aberdeen wholesale bookseller and stationer, has left a graphic account of the execution in his unpublished memoirs. As a boy he was gripped by a mixture of curiosity and pity. He pointed out that sheep-stealing had become so common the judges resolved 'to make an example of the first well authenticated case'. He believed that if Grant had not committed suicide he would have hanged, not 'poor Ritchie'.

'Aberdeen went into mourning', wrote Smith in the late 19th century, 'shutting up places of business and going into the country to escape the exhibition that was to vindicate the majesty of the law, and deter offenders from breaking it in all future time. Although participating in the universal feeling of pity for the criminal my curiosity to see the tragedy was too strong to overcome, and I witnessed the whole scene'.

He went on: 'The scaffold projected into Castle Street - the appearance upon it of the ruddy-faced innocent looking lad, in his graveclothes, and him yet living - the universal sigh that ran through the crowd when the chaplain began the devotional exercises (it was Mr. Thom, master of Gordon's Hospital who held the office) - the sobs that mingled with the singing of the psalm by the crowd - the kind large-hearted Professor Kidd, as he stood by him to the last, and the bustling movements of the executioner (John Milne himself a criminal) the step upon the Drop, the bang when it fell and the cries that would be held no longer, left an impression on my mind that can never be effaced'.

Cutting edge. The blade of the Aberdeen 'Maiden'.
(From 'This Braif Toun').

Traffic exhaust fumes have replaced the stench of burning witches in Commerce Street, Aberdeen. Executions took place in the hollow between Heading Hill (left) and Castle Hill.

'The Mids o' Mar'. The 17th century keep-tower photographed from Lodge Walk.

(Photo courtesy: Aberdeen City Council Publicity and Promotions Division).

Chapter Ten

Bon-Accord Gothic

They called it 'Ordeal by Blood'. If a murderer was undiscovered in the community neighbours would gather to touch the corpse. If the corpse bled at the nose, or mouth, or from its wound, the person who touched it was the guilty party.

In October 1698 the minister's wife at Slains, near Collieston, was found dead in bed. Suspicion fell on her stepson, although there was no sign of violence. Had she been poisoned? To find the answer to the mystery her body was laid out in full view. The minister offered a prayer then all present touched the corpse, but without any firm conclusion.

In Aberlour, the naked body of a woman was carried to the gate of the churchyard. When forced to approach the body her murderer blurted out his guilt. It was her son.

There was a hint of this curious North-east superstition at an Aberdeenshire farmer's funeral in August 1821.

When George Thom was asked to view the body of his brother-in-law, William Mitchell, he refused point-blank, No wonder, perhaps, for Thom had deliberately poisoned the man.

Sixty-one-year-old Thom, who farmed Harthill in the Garioch, was said to be respectable with an irreproachable character.

After his wife died he wed Jean Mitchell, who spent her spinsterhood with her two brothers, James and William, and two sisters, Helen and Mary, at their home at Burnside, in the parish of Keig, near Alford. They were an honest and God-fearing family. They were also well off for the times. At first fate had smiled kindly on the Mitchells. A brother had left them a tidy windfall in his will and Jean was already a wealthy woman by the time she wed Thom.

Thom planned to get his hands on the Mitchells' money and property and devised an evil plot to murder them. He decided to carry out the deed during a rare, solo visit to Burnside on the eve of Sacramental Sunday.

The Mitchells welcomed Thom with open arms and that night they took supper before retiring.

Thom made an excuse to sleep in the kitchen because he claimed he had business at Mains of Cluny the next morning and wanted an early start. But the Mitchells would not hear of it. In the wee small hours of Sunday morning James Mitchell, who slept in the kitchen, heard the shuffle of feet near a cupboard. But the shutters of his box-bed were shut and he did not check on the person's identity.

If he had been inquisitive he may have caught Thom red-handed, slipping arsenic into the salt cellar.

But his sister Helen showed more curiosity when she and Thom were alone in the kitchen the next morning. He refused her offer of breakfast, making the excuse he wanted on the road before the churchgoers appeared.

Helen watched as Thom shook some crumbs of bread and cheese on a table. She noticed something white. She questioned Thom about the substance, but he made no reply and took to the road with a chunk of bread given by William.

At the Mains of Cluny he ate a hearty breakfast. But on the road to Harthill he had a strange conversation with a gentleman whom he knew. He complained of having been ill. He blamed it on eating something at Mains of Cluny, or Burnside. If he had not used a crow's feather to induce vomiting, he said, he might not be alive to tell the tale. That was his story.

The lie, no doubt, weighed heavily on the minds of the jury when Thom stood trial at the Circuit Court in Aberdeen in September.

Back at Burnside meanwhile Mary Mitchell prepared a milk pottage for breakfast. In court her brother James said he had not cared for the pottage that fateful morning. He complained that it had a 'sweetish sickening taste'. But William ate heartily enough and his sisters tasted nothing unusual. James became ill as he dressed for kirk. His condition worsened but he decided to walk to the church, even though he felt himself 'turning blind'. James's agony continued. He staggered from the church building to find William violently sick in the churchyard. Even so William went into the service, while his brother somehow made his way back home, vomiting several times by the wayside.

The physical condition of the Mitchells, brothers and sisters, worsened, James complained of the lower part of his body 'burning within'. William, back home from the kirk, was in agony with a 'swelling in his breast, rising to his throat'. His eyesight, too,

68

was affected.

Helen and Mary fared no better. By the Monday, Helen could 'scarcely feel the ground below her' because her feet were numb. A burning pain stabbed her heart and she suffered a 'great thirst'. Even by the time of Thom's trial she had still not fully recovered. Mary had no feeling in her legs, from her knee joints downwards.

William's condition had deteriorated alarmingly. He was almost blind and he had all but lost the power of his arms, He lingered for a week before dying the following Sunday. James told the court: 'He rose to look for a drink, returned to his bed, stretched himself - and gave a terrible groan, then lay quiet'.

James broke down in the witness box when he described how he went to his sisters and told them: 'William is gaen to wear awa' out among us'.

It transpired that the Mitchells had suspected Thom was behind their mystery illness but, incredibly, had decided to keep quiet in the hope they would make a complete recovery.

George Thom and his wife attended William's funeral, although they were not welcome. Their very presence was an embarrassment to the family and other mourners. Even some of the neighbours informed James Mitchell if the Thoms remained they would leave, which indicates the Mitchells had spoken their minds.

'The Black Kalendar of Aberdeen' touches on the 'Ordeal of Blood' superstition thus: 'Before they went away, Helen Mitchell bade her sister (Thom's wife) go and look at the corpse, which she did, but Thom did not.

'We do not know whether or not there was any superstitious notion in Helen Mitchell's mind when she bade her sister look on the dead body, but in all probability there was in Thom's when he avoided approaching it, a dread of undergoing an ordeal, of which such extraordinary relations are on record'.

In court it was said that Thom's wife had told him: 'Nelly says my brother was poisoned'.

Thom resurrected another misguided belief in reply. He suggested that toads and puddocks (frogs) in the burn were responsible for the poison. But Helen Mitchell would have none of it, saying the pottage had been made with milk and not water.

Thom and his wife were arrested in bed, but Jean was later released.

During the lengthy trial - the first day's evidence ended at 2am the following morning - it emerged that a man resembling Thom had bought arsenic from a druggist in Aberdeen, allegedly to kill rats.

Thom was found guilty on circumstantial evidence. He continued to deny his guilt in the death cell. But, with all hope of a respite gone, he signed a confession, vindicating his wife. His execution was set for Friday, November 16, 1821.

A rumour tormented Thom during his last days. A report swept Aberdeen that he was the killer of Thomas Gill, whose body was found floating in the harbour in November 1817. Thom said he was ignorant of the crime, as he was confined to his sick bed at the time.

On the day of his execution Thom was brought into the lobby of the courthouse at two o'clock. His shroud was put on and his arms pinioned.

In the courthouse itself he thanked magistrates for their humane treatment. The man was unable to stand and sat in a chair while Reverend Dr Kidd offered a prayer.

Dr Kidd and Reverend Thom supported the condemned man as they walked to the scaffold. George Thom had requested that part of the 103rd Psalm be sung, and the voices had barely faded in the afternoon air when Thom was turned off at five minutes to three, dying without a struggle.

But there would be little hope of a blessed resurrection of Thom. His corpse was cut down and then escorted by the Aberdeenshire Militia to the Marischal College where Doctors Skene and Ewing waited to carry out an experiment.

It could have been a scene torn from the pages of a Gothic horror story. Frock-coated surgeons stooped over a bloodless corpse in a gloomy anatomical chamber. A lantern glimmering on the paraphernalia of their galvanic experiment...a heavy battery charged with a dilute solution of nitric and sulphuric acids from which dangled wires with pointed metal rods.

Readers of the 'Aberdeen Journal' were given details of Thom's execution and the hour-long experiment in the next edition. Under the heading, 'Galvanic Phenomena' they were told;-

'The upper part of the spinal cord and the sciatic nerve were immediately laid bare, and a Galvanic Arc was then established, by applying the positive wire to the Spine, and the negative to the Sciatic Nerve, when a general convulsive starting of the body was produced'.

When the apparatus was applied elsewhere to the corpse: 'The

70

hand was closed with such violence as to resist the exertions of one of the assistants to keep it open'.

Here was a faint echo of a controversial galvanic experiment carried out by Glasgow surgeons on the corpse of a hanged criminal in 1818, the year Mary Shelley's classic tale of terror, 'Frankenstein', first appeared.

Murderer Matthew Clydesdale's body was linked to a Voltaic pile with ghastly results for some of the spectators. The dead man's chest heaved and fell, as if he were still alive, and a leg shot out with such force that a medical student was almost sent flying. Clydesdale's lifeless features twitched in apparent rage, horror, despair, anguish - and ghastly grins. It proved too much for some non-medical gentlemen who fled the room, terrified and sickened. (In 1803 a beadle died of fright after a galvanic experiment on a man hanged in Newgate).

There was no such disturbance by those who attended the Aberdeen experiment. But it is not known how many remained to see George Thom's corpse dissected!

Chapter Eleven

Fallen Hero

On a moonlit moor, near Midmar Lodge in Aberdeenshire, an English bull terrier pioneered today's police dog work when its master turned it loose on a gang of whisky smugglers.

It happened on February 8,1816, and the black and tan terrier became a fighting fury as it scattered the gang and their four pack horses laden with illicit booze. The dog was trained to seize a horse by the nose, forcing the terrified beast to shed its load.

History has not left us the name of the remarkable dog, but its master was the colourful Malcolm Gillespie, who, next to Rabbie Burns, was probably the most famous Scottish Exciseman ever.

Gillespie who came from Dunblane, began his working life as a soldier. For three years he served as a recruiting officer at Brechin for the first regiment of foot. In that time he recruited '400 fine young lads' to the colours.

He entered the Excise service at the age of 20. Within a short period he had built a formidable reputation for himself by smashing the trade of contraband liquor smuggled from the Continent into East of Scotland ports. His book of seizures was fat and it grew fatter as he became the terror of the whisky smugglers. His operations, begun in Collieston in 1807, spread to Stonehaven, and later to the notorious Skene Ride, a wild, desolate stretch of countryside between Dee and Don.

Gillespie the gauger was at the centre of several running battles with the smugglers and if his exploits are true he escaped death on more than one occasion.

In a pitched battle at the Hill of Auchronie, his horse lost an eye. So in 1816 he decided to enlist the help of a dog. He bought a 'bull terrier' at considerable expense from the equally colourful Captain Robert Barclay Allardice of Ury, keep-fit fanatic, and patron of boxing who trained champion bare knuckle fighters John Gully and Tom Cribb at his estate outside Stonehaven. Captain Bob was the toast of the 'Fancy' and no mean athlete. At the age of

20 he lifted an 18 stone man from the floor to table with one hand.

But his most legendary exploit was winning a 1,000 guinea wager by walking 1,000 miles in 1,000 successive hours at Newmarket - and in a top hat, too!

Gillespie prized the dog highly. He told an acquaintance he valued the dog above everything and 'would not have disposed of it for 100 guineas'.

Unfortunately, the dog's career was short-lived. After putting smugglers to flight at Midmar and Cottown of Kintore it was shot dead by a Highlander during a skirmish at Parkhill on the banks of the Don. When Gillespie's property was rouped after his death a hound bitch and a doghouse and collar were sold for a total of £1 3s 6d.

But the gauger's extravagant life-style and the costs of running a household at Crombie Cottage, Skene, and a large number of servants, forced him to turn to a life of crime. Gillespie had married at 20 and had children 'whom he deeply loved'.

He was described by friends as being 'generous to a fault'.

He enlisted the dubious skills of his private secretary George Skene Edwards to carry out a series of daring frauds by forging and uttering 22 different bills.

They adopted the names of local farmers, and Edwards traced some of their signatures on a window pane.

The amount involved was £554 and 10 shillings. They grew careless and some of the signatures were of people either in the infirmary or dead.

Before the fraud was revealed Gillespie sunk to a new low. He decided to retrieve his ruined fortunes by defrauding insurance companies by staging a fire at Crombie Cottage.

The gauger had insured his home for £530 with the Palladium Insurance Company, London, and for £300 with the Phoenix Company.

Sometime before the blaze a quantity of gunpowder was placed in the barn and some tow and rosin put in the cellar.

The date set for the crime was the night of February 21, 1827, when Gillespie was in Edinburgh on business. Two of his daughters were at Crombie Cottage but did not take part in what followed.

Before leaving Gillespie called together his housekeeper, Jessy Greig, George Skene Edwards and his brother John and William Jenkins.

The sly Gillespie did not speak plainly of his intentions but said there would be 'no harm' in burning the house as it would 'take him out of his present difficulties'.

A nod was as good as a wink. On the day before the fire John Edwards and another servant George Brownie, smeared melted rosin on the furniture and placed sticks of the stuff between the joists of the house. They also sprinkled gunpowder and turpentine on floors. Brownie trimmed the thatch on the roof between the west room and the other parts of the house for it was intended to save the west room.

The Edwards brothers left about seven o'clock in the evening while Jenkins went to his bed in the stable loft, his accomplices promising to waken him when 'the thing should be set a-going'.

They did as promised and when they gathered in the cottage Jessy Greig gave each a dram for their troubles.

Brownie lit two candles and gave one to Lexy Campbell, a servant for 13 years, who went off to the cellar. Brownie went into a room and set fire to tow.

Crombie Cottage was burned to the ground. Gillespie, on his return, was delighted with the result and said the thing had been 'genteelly done'.

The gauger was arrested on April 30. He told the messenger: 'Good God, I'm a gone man. Let me get out of the way for a short time and I will put it right'.

At the Circuit Court in Aberdeen in September Gillespie and George Edwards were charged with uttering and fraud.

During the 15-hour trial Brownie, Greig and Campbell tried to throw the blame of the crimes on George Edwards, But the court could see through their ploy. Gillespie was found guilty of eight of the charges of forgery and uttering and was sentenced to death - the verdict delivered by the jury in an envelope with a tell-tale black seal.

If Gillespie had been acquitted he would have still faced the charges of fire-raising with intent to defraud.

The judges, Lord Pitmilly and Galloway, in passing sentence, referred to Gillespie's altered circumstances.

Lord Pitmilly told the prisoner: 'The recollection of these things has not been absent from our minds one single moment since the trial began, and I can scarcely make myself believe such a reverse has taken place'.

Lord Galloway told the condemned man he should 'not look for mercy in this world'.

Edwards was found guilty of forgery only but after objections the case was certified for the opinion of the High Court.

Edwards later pleaded guilty in Edinburgh to the charge of forgery and was sentenced to transportation for life.

After Gillespie was sentenced in Aberdeen George Brownie and Lexy Campbell were then placed at the bar, They admitted charges of fire-raising and were sentenced to seven years' transportation.

Gillespie, who was 50, was not a popular figure in the Highlands for obvious reasons, and it was rumoured that a band of Highland smugglers, wearing tartan and headed by a piper, would attend his execution on Friday, 16 November 1827. It was a false rumour.

In his death cell the battling gauger showed jailers 42 wounds inflicted on various parts of his body during his 28 years as an Exciseman. He also took time to write his memoirs and dying declaration.

On the eve of his execution he took leave of his family. He slept peacefully enough for a man about to hang. In the old courthouse, a few yards from the scaffold, Gillespie sipped a glass of water as he gave details of his forgeries to the magistrates, protesting his intentions were honest. He walked to the scaffold 'with a firm and steady step'.

The huge crowd fell silent as he took his place on the drop. There was a touching moment when he fixed his gaze westward, towards Skene, with a 'peculiarly melancholy expression'. He gave the signal to the hangman, and died with 'little if any struggle'.

One mystery remains. After Gillespie's body was cut down it was taken to Skene where it was buried in the local kirkyard.

At the beginning of this century a curious sexton exhumed the famous exciseman's coffin. It contained only stones!

Gillespie's corpse may have been stolen by resurrectionists - grave robbers! The deed could have been done before interment. Why else fill the coffin with stones to give the impression a body was still inside?

A fantastic solution to the mystery might be that Gillespie had somehow managed to 'cheat the widdie' and was still breathing when cut down!

Chapter Twelve

Mrs Humphrey's Ordeal

O*it's a sair thing to wash for the gibbet; but I hope I will be washed in the blood of the Redeemer.*

Poor Mrs Humphrey. They were not the last words she spoke on her last day on earth. But though she committed a heinous crime - pouring vitriol into her sleeping husband's gaping mouth - the last woman to hang in Aberdeen certainly suffered terribly in the courtroom and the scaffold.

The facts are that Mrs Humphrey, born Catherine Davidson at Keith-Hall, near Inverurie, had been wed for 33 years before she killed her husband. The first half of married life with Englishman James Humphrey, flesher and professional soldier, was pure bliss, marred by the death of their infant child.

Catherine, who had moved into town as a bairn, had met Humphrey while he served with the Windsor Foresters fencible light cavalry in Aberdeen. He would also wear the uniform of the Aberdeenshire Militia, a regiment whose duties included guarding the scaffold at executions.

Cracks appeared in their marriage when they both took to drink. They would appear to have been their own best customers at the public house they ran in Albion Street, in the East End of Aberdeen. In 1830, the year of Mrs Humphrey's execution, it had previously been called the Bowl Road - the ancient 'Bool-gait', which led eastwards from Park Road to the Links. The Police Commissioners agreed on a name change in the vain hope a stroke of a pen would alter the notorious character of the street.

The couple were at each other's throats continually. They quarrelled in front of friends and servants.

Catherine suspected her husband was unfaithful and was often heard to threaten his life.

A witness told the Autumn Circuit Court how Humphrey, during a blazing row, tilted his neck and taunted his wife: 'There, do it now, for you will do it sometime!'.

Humphrey made a chilling prediction - his wife, he said, would end her days 'looking down Marischal Street', a reference to being hanged on the Castlegate gallows.

Their feuding grew bitter until the night of Friday, April 16, 1830, when Catherine decided to carry out the deed.

First, she did an unusual thing - she ordered the servant to go to bed before her. The servant overheard her mistress say: 'Lord God, if anybody would give him poison, and keep my hand clear of it'.

The servant had barely closed her eyes when Mrs Humphrey came to her on her stocking soles and said her husband had taken ill, and was making noises. Her mistress *had a smile on her face as she spoke'*.

Humphrey was writhing in agony. 'I'm burned! I'm gone! I'm roasted!', he roared from his death bed.

Catherine tried to calm him by saying he must have had a 'bad drink'.

'Oh, woman, woman', gasped Humphrey, having none of it, 'whatever I have gotten, it was in my own house. You have tried to do this often, and you have done it now'.

Three glasses stood on the table. There had only been two when the servant retired. A phial which had contained three or four teaspoonfuls of vitriol was empty. Humphrey's bed clothes were burned. And when a child in the room put the glass to its lips it cried out in pain.

A doctor was summoned but there was little he could do. Humphrey died on the Sunday morning and with his dying breath he absolved his wife of the crime.

But the jury would not be swayed. After the trial which began at noon and ended at midnight, Catherine was found guilty of murder. Lord Mackenzie's sentence was death, following by dissection.

The good judge showed no mercy to the stout, middle-aged woman standing at the bar. 'You will appear before God stained with the blood of a murdered husband', he thundered. Catherine's face, good looking in its day, sagged: 'Oh, no my lord' she sobbed, 'I didna do't-oh, no, no...'

On the eve of her execution she confessed her guilt, saying 'she had been driven by jealously and malice excited by the misconduct of her husband and dislike he bore towards her'. She admitted that she had been in such a state of mind when receiving the 'awful sentence' she did not hear it.

There was little rest for Catherine in the condemned cell. She could hear the carpenters build her gallows in Castle Street. Each hammer blow must have sounded like another nail in her coffin, although she would have no known grave.

At 2.30 in the afternoon of Friday, October 8th, Catherine was led from the East Prison on the arms of her jailers. The first stop was the old courthouse where the Lord Provost and magistrates were gathered in all their dignity.

Psalms were sung, including the 51st Psalm, known in hanging circles as 'the neck verse', the gloomy melody of martyrs, part of which the Montrose murderer Mrs Shuttleworth objected to.

Drink, Catherine told the assembled City Fathers, was her downfall. (Did they heed her warning as they gathered in the nearby Lemon Tree Hotel for a post-execution dram?)

In a clear, firm voice she went on: 'Gentlemen, you who have it in your power should look to the public houses in the quarter where I lived for many of them are in a bad state and have much need to be looked after'.

Expressing a desire that the world would take warning by her case Reverend Dr Kidd, who had prayed with Catherine in the condemned cell, endorsed what she had said, adding: 'That if such houses were not put down there would be a desolation of society'. (This warning appears to have gone unheeded for by 1837 Aberdeen, with a population of just 60,000, had 870 premises where drink could be bought. There was one public house for every 11 families living in the parish of Greyfriars).

Catherine, 'genteely dressed' in black, was close to fainting when she was placed on the drop by the new hangman, John Scott. She never once lifted her eyes to look around at the huge crowd that pressed around the scaffold and stretched back as far as St Katherine's Wynd in Union Street.

She dropped her handkerchief as a signal to Scott, who 'proceeded to do his duty'. Her last words were: 'Oh, my God...' And at five minutes to three the drop fell.

Mrs Humphrey's long ordeal was almost over. From the time she was taken from her cell to the moment the drop fell 25 minutes had elapsed. By 1922 the time scale from cell to scaffold was 10 seconds.

But even then Catherine appeared not to be out of her suffering. Her body convulsed at the end of the rope and twice she raised her hands 'in the attitude of supplication'. The crowd grew restless. But they melted away quietly enough. The corpse hung for 40 minutes before it was taken away to Marischal College where the anatomist Dr Pirrie waited patiently with a group of 'students and private professional people'. Mrs Humphrey was the last hanged criminal to be handed over for dissection in the city.

But the tragic tale of Catherine Humphrey has a harrowing footnote.

It centres on a woman who died on the Aberdeen scaffold the previous century.

Jean Craig, a habitual thief, and Elspet Reid, from Banffshire, appeared before Lords Gardenstone and Braxfield (of 'Weir of Hermiston' fame, who once told a smooth-tongued accused: 'You're a very clever chiel, man - but ye would be none the waur o' a hanging') at Aberdeen Circuit Court in May 1784.

Jean was accused of stealing cloth from the bleachfield at Huntly. Elspet was accused of housebreaking and theft aggravated by being a reputed thief. They both received the death sentence but won brief respites by claiming to be pregnant.

Craig hanged in Aberdeen in July 1784, while Reid was executed the following January.

What has this to do with Catherine Humphrey?

To quote a local scribe after her hanging: 'It is a singular fact and one which Mrs Humphrey more than once mentioned since her trial, that being present at Jean Craig's execution on the body being cut down, the rope was, as was then usual, thrown among the crowd, when the knot struck her on the breast.

'She said she recoiled with horror and that the circumstances had borne much on her mind since she received her sentence'.

This would mean Mrs Humphrey, who was about 50 at the time of her death, would have been only five years old at the time of that fateful incident. A bit young to be in a crowd scrambling for souvenirs at a hanging! But, true or otherwise, perhaps it was a salutary tale for the folk of the auld Bool Road, name change or not.

Interior of the Aberdeen Tolbooth's condemned cell, showing the 'lang gade'.
(Photo courtesy: Aberdeen City Council Publicity and Promotions Division).

An iron yett in the Tolbooth. It looks impregnable, but it could not hold Peter Young and his gang.
(Photo courtesy: Aberdeen City Council Publicity and Promotions Division).

Sketch of Malcolm Gillespie, the famous exciseman, hanged for forgery at Aberdeen in November 1827.

On the warpath! Peter Williamson dressed as an American Indian. He successfully hounded his Aberdeen 'kidnappers'.
(Courtesy: Robert Smith).

Chapter Thirteen

Salmon Meg and Others

A Highland soldier, billeted at Castlehill Barracks in 1832, wrote of Aberdeen's prostitution problem:-

'In no town in which I have been stationed have I ever observed that portion of the community dominated 'street walkers' enjoy such unbounded licence'.

The soldier, a private in the 72nd - (the Duke of Albany's Own Highlanders, later the Seaforths) - went on in his letter: 'At all hours of the day, every day of the week, and in every street of the city, they perambulate, or rather, prowl, not singly but in bands, insulting any woman they meet'.

He said they had obtained 'complete possession' of the East End, extending from Park Lane to the head of King Street.

'Might not the Police do more to eradicate this nuisance', he lamented.

Being a seaport and garrison town Aberdeen had a profusion of brothels and prostitutes in the middle of the 19th century.

One of the largest was Morris O'Conner's in Fredrick Street, which housed 34 women.

John Chisholm's brothel at the rear of the Weigh-house at the harbour bore the saucy soubriquet, the 'Dundee Dock'.

In 1840 there were 72 organised brothels, and 500 known prostitutes plying their trade. It was estimated that disease weakened their health after only six weeks and as many as 90 women died every year.

Trouble was never far away. Thirteen years after the soldier's lamentations a band of prostitutes managed to stir up an ugly situation between Irish troops and townsfolk. It almost erupted in a repeat of the notorious Plainstones Massacre of 1802.

On a dark wintry night in February 1845 off-duty members of the 88th Regiment (Connaught Rangers), accompanied by a number of prostitutes from Shore Brae, marched down Marischal Street, smelling of drink and looking for trouble.

On reaching the bridge over Virginia Street they began pelting pedestrians below with stones and other missiles.

An angry crowd locked horns with the soldiers and began beating them. Police reinforced by 'specials' from the Shore Porters arrived on the scene.

The soldiers beat a hasty retreat to Castlehill Barracks, leaving several of their comrades in the hands of the mob. The situation grew serious when reinforcements arrived from the barracks. The new arrivals were armed with rifles with fixed bayonets. After seven soldiers were released into the custody of their comrades the situation cooled. The disgraced soldiers were dealt with leniently at the Police Court and less than three months later the regiment packed its kitbags and sailed for Eniskillen.

A week or so later the 60th Rifles (King's Royal Rifle Corps) took their place, but soon enraged the populace by throwing a cordon of sentries around the Links whenever they trained.

The 'Braif Toun' of Aberdeen was seldom touched with such madness, but there were other disturbances involving prostitutes.

In June 1815, King George III's birthday - ironically the anniversary of the Plainstones Massacre - was the catalyst of a raid on an infamous town brothel.

A screaming mob of 500 persons attacked Meggie Dick's house of ill-repute. 'The White Ship', a great favourite with visiting seamen.

After smashing down the front door the mob gutted the premises, heaping the furniture in the gutter and setting it alight.

Mistress Meggie and her good ladies did not escape their wrath. They were brutally manhandled and their caps torn from their heads.

At the Circuit Court in September four young lads appeared on trial on charges of mobbing, rioting and assault. John Douglas, Donald Mackay and Arthur Smollett were found guilty of mobbing and rioting. The ringleader Douglas was sentenced to seven year's transportation, while the other two were confined in the Bridewell for a year. Alexander Burr, the fourth accused, was dismissed.

About 1830 the Aberdeen mob beseiged another well-known brothel, Salmon Meg's, in the St Nicholas Street district.

The house was stripped of its furniture and 'The Black Kalendar of Aberdeen' describes how a vandal 'bestrode Margaret's eight day clock, as it lay on its back unconsciously on the street, and, a good axe in his hand, deliberately hewed it into pieces'.

But there was a less amusing end to the incident in Margaret Creek's 'house of bad fame' on a night in September 1807.

Revenge was in the air when a party of soldiers of the Argyleshire Militia, garrisoned at Castlehill, were given special leave to go out on the town. They wore side-arms and at about one or two in the morning they arrived at the door of the brothel in Justice Port.

Their intended victim was inside. He was 'The Black Drummer' - John Simpson - who was in Aberdeen on a recruiting drive for the 29th Regiment.

'The Black Drummer', a huge black fellow with a powerful set of fists, as their comrades knew to their cost, had made an enemy of the Argyleshire men. It seemed he showed up from time to time at Castlehill Barracks and challenged soldiers to fight.

Tragically, on one occasion he accidentally killed a soldier. Simpson had rushed forward to meet his challenger, thrust his head between his opponent's legs, hoisted him on his broad shoulders, before dashing him to the ground. The man's skull shattered like an egg.

When the men of the Argyleshire Militia knocked on Meg Creek's door, demanding drink, they could hear Simpson's voice from within. They began taunting 'The Black Drummer' and threw stones at Meg's windows.

Simpson was a brave fellow and raced out into the street to face his tormentors. He was instantly flattened with a blow to the head by a flying stone. Somehow he managed to stagger back indoors. Smelling blood his assailants followed him.

In the dark, unlit rooms the militiamen drew their bayonets. They believed Simpson was hiding under the bedclothes in a room and plunged the bayonets into the blankets, to no avail.

Furiously, they hunted him down. They eventually found Simpson collapsed in a heap behind the front door of the brothel. They dragged him outside and when Simpson's body was found in the gutter it was dreadfully mangled and had been stabbed many times. His skull was fractured in two places and a bayonet thrust had pierced his heart.

In January 1808 three soldiers, Donald Macallum, Daniel MacPherson and James Graham, stood trial for the murder of 'The Black Drummer'. But there was much confusion as a result of the prosecution calling on two witnesses with criminal backgrounds - namely, Meg Creek and Peter Skinner, who had been pilloried and whipped for robbing a dead body at Aberdeen Beach. There was an adjournment while the defence objections were considered, then quashed. But seeds of doubt were sown in the minds of the jury and the charges were found not proven.

'Riding the Stang' was a punishment usually reserved for adulterers and wife beaters.

It involved mounting the offender astride a rough pole or tree trunk and carrying him, none too gently, around the streets. During meal mob riots in Aberdeen in the middle of the 18th century a meal merchant managed to escape the indignity at the hands of unruly apprentices.

Aberdeen's music halls were also the target for hooliganism.

On Friday, April 5, 1889, a gala night at the Bon-Accord Music Hall turned into a riot when a popular act failed to turn up. The band fled as hooligans hurled music stands and chairs onto the stage and the air became a blizzard of music sheets.

The footlights were turned off and artistes fled in the darkness as baton-wielding police made a number of arrests.

The Bon-Accord Music Hall never opened its doors again. The former variety hall, and one time United Free Church, stood next door to the Prince of Wales public house in St Nicholas Lane, until it was demolished in 1993.

By the end of the last century there were no brothels in the city and the number of prostitutes was reduced to less than 50.

This was due to a massive street clean-up operation by the zealous and ever vigilant Chief Constable, Tam Wyness, the son of a Midmar farmer, whose popularity in certain quarters of the licensed trade earned him the nickname, 'The Terror of the Trade', and a poetic lampoon, 'The New Dictator', which appeared in the weekly newspaper, 'Bon-Accord'.

But at least Chief Constable Wyness did not tackle prostitution with the painful methods employed by the magistrates of the burgh in the 15th century.

In April 1497 when 'the strange sickness of Nappilis' - venereal disease - was introduced into Aberdeen by followers of Perkin Warbeck, self-styled Duke of York, the brothels were emptied and prostitutes branded on the cheek with a 'het yrne', and then banished.

Chapter Fourteen

The Boyndlie Murder

Boyndlie farm servant James Burnett was described by friends and family as a 'kind and attentive' husband. He had been married for more than quarter-a-century and helped raise four sons and three daughters.

Yet Burnett, who was 44-years-old, cold-heartedly poisoned his invalid wife so that he'd be free to marry a lass 20 years younger than himself.

Burnett and his wife, Margaret, several years his senior, walked with the aid of a crutch because of a stroke which had left her paralysed down her left side.

They virtually lived separate lives for almost two years before he plotted her agonising death.

Mrs Burnett lived in a small croft at Shelmanae (today it is called Skelmanae), in the parish of Tyrie, eight miles south-west of Fraserburgh. Her husband worked and lived at Mr Pittendrigh's farm of Protshaugh, less than a mile's walk across the fields.

Mrs Burnett lived at Shelmanae with her daughter Margaret and son, Thomas, the rest of the family apparently having left home.

Her estranged husband shared his bed in a house in Protshaugh Farm with Jean Carty, a maid of 23 or 24 years of age.

Burnett told the quine they would marry as soon as his invalid wife died. Little did she imagine the demons that tormented her lover.

On the evening of Wednesday, November 2, 1848, Burnett called at Shelmanae where his sickly wife was bed-ridden. He said he had been given some powders by the family doctor, Dr Wood, to take 'the stuff off her stomach'.

Although Mrs Burnett expressed no desire for the medicine her husband gave it to her - mixing the powders in a tea cup with jelly and sugar.

Their daughter Margaret was in the room and saw her mother drink the medicine. The girl was ordered to bed by her father, who said he would spend the night at Shelmanae. But Margaret, no doubt worried about her mother's condition, or perhaps she suspected something, returned to the room to find her mother violently sick.

Burnett asked his wife if he should fetch 'that cratur', meaning the doctor. But the dying woman cried out: 'I am poisoned! I am poisoned! God reward them upon earth for what they have done to me!'.

Margaret, giving evidence at the Spring Circuit Court of 1849, said her father 'seemed not very much concerned about her mother', who was in great agony. Strichen and New Pitsligo were only a few miles away and there was a 'good horse in the stable', yet Burnett did not fetch a doctor.

Burnett made a queer statement at Shelmanae, saying he had accidently smashed a cup which had contained his wife's medicine. He had no doubt attempted to get rid of the evidence.

Margaret described how her mother 'grew very death-like' and died just after six on Thursday morning.

There was little time for mourning at Shelmanae. The following day, Friday, November 4, poor Mrs Burnett was hustled to her grave in the kirkyard at Strichen.

If that was not enough to set tongues wagging in the north-west corner of Buchan there was an even bigger scandal to follow.

Mrs Burnett was barely cold in her tomb when within a week or two after her funeral the banns of marriage between Burnett and Jean Carty were proclaimed at the parish church in Tyrie, St Andrews, a pretty kirk, built in 1800, with a birdcage bellcote above the west door. Burnett, and his bride-to-be could hardly have failed to notice the grim tombstone which lies directly outside the door. It is a 17th century tombstone with macabre carvings of skull and human bones - an omen, indeed!

In December the law in the shape of county policeman James Forsyth appeared on Burnett's doorstop at Protshaugh, and asked some awkward questions about his wife's death. (I spoke to Charles Lowe, of Memsie, whose great-grandfather John Lowe, a stone mason, was rudely awakened by two policemen and ordered to show them the lights of Protshaugh. John would not be rushed, insisting he be warmly attired before facing the cold night air!).

Constable Forsyth suggested Burnett should arrange to have his wife's body examined by two medical gentlemen, but Burnett hedged, saying he could not bear the idea. Forsyth told him he need not be present, as he might employ others. Forsyth lost patience when Burnett said he could not afford the expense. The policeman told him the Procurator Fiscal would do it at public expense.

Burnett replied: 'Oh, I don't think it - I don't know well what to bid you say'.

Forsyth told the court in Aberdeen: 'I gave information to the Fiscal next day; my enquiry was just in consequence of what I heard in the country. I enquired if arsenic had been sold in the shops of Pitsligo lately, but found there had been none sold for a twelve month'.

The scene switched to the graveyard at Strichen Parish Church, an 18th century harled rectangle of a building, where gravediggers disinterred Mrs Burnett's coffin on December 16.

The coffin was carried inside the church where Dr Gavin performed a post mortem examination on her body. The stomach and its contents and part of the liver and oesophagus were sealed in bottles and dispatched to the Crown Agent's Office in Edinburgh for analysis.

'The internal appearance of the stomach was consistent with death by arsenic', said Dr Gavin.

The Crown scientists collected 23 grains of arsenic from the contents of the stomach.

A vital witness, Elizabeth Macdonald, who ran posts between Tyrie and Fraserburgh, was approached by Burnett on the Sunday before his wife's death.

He asked Macdonald to go some errands for him in Fraserburgh. He gave her money for a New Testament and some stationery. He hesitated no doubt over his third request. 'He did not know if it was fair or not', it was said by the witness. 'If it was not a fair one she would not go', was the gist of Macdonald's response.

Burnett explained to her that he was troubled with a 'great deal of rottans' (rats) in his house and over his head at night. She bought threepence worth of arsenic from George McDonald, the druggist in Fraserburgh. It was tied up in three papers and labelled, 'Poison'. She gave the arsenic to Burnett on her return.

Burnett's bride-to-be was next to give evidence. Jean Carty, showing considerable reluctance, was asked by the defence:-

Was it agreed between you and the prisoner, before his wife's death, that you were to be married after she died?—

Witness (hesitantly)—Yes.

Q. Did the prisoner say anything to you about his wife when you were speaking about being married?

A. He said that if she did not get well now she would not be long to the fore.

Q. Did he ever ask you when his wife was alive, to go away and live with him somewhere else?

A. Yes.

Q. Was it some place where you were not known?

A. Yes.

Q. And to be married?

A. I don't recollect.

Q. Did you agree to his proposal?

A. No - I refused.

Q. You were proclaimed shortly after his wife's death?

A. Yes, at the church of Tyrie.

Q. Were you on terms of intimacy with Burnett before his wife's death?

A. Yes.

Q. Was the room in which you slept near that in which the prisoner slept?

A. It was no just terrible far.

Q. Did you ever, on any occasion, leave your own room and go into the one where Burnett slept?

A. I had no errand there.

Q. I am not asking whether you had any errand. I am asking whether you left your own room at night and went into the room where Burnett slept?

A. Yes.

Q. Was he in bed at the time?

A. Yes.

The jury, when it retired, took only five minutes to reach their verdict-guilty. Lord Mackenzie then put on the black cap and pronounced the death sentence on Burnett, 'The Boyndlie Murderer'.

During the trial Burnett left the bar for a drink of water. He asked court officers how they viewed the case. 'It looks very black', they told him. When Burnett asked what was the blackest points, he was met with blank stares.

The date of his execution was Tuesday, May 22 1849.

On the appointed day Burnett slept for three hours during the night and was joined in prayers at five in the morning by Mr Strahan, the prison chaplain, who found him in a 'very satisfactory state of mind'. At six Burnett managed to breakfast on bread and tea. Reverend Dr Mackintosh engaged Burnett in 'devotional exercises'.

The reporter from the 'Aberdeen Journal' meantime noted: 'The scaffold was erected at an early hour and (though there was little 'clank' of carpenters' hammers, as the whole apparatus is fastened together by screws) the glare of the flaring artificial lights, the steelness of the morning, and the gloomy appearance of the fatal apparatus, are described by those who witnessed the scene as having a peculiarly striking and ghastly effect'.

In his cell Burnett and the ministers sang, 'The Hour of My Departure's Come', and shortly after eight the hangman appeared and pinioned Burnett's arms.

As the procession moved through the passage under the courthouse Burnett resolved to 'shut his eyes' during the remaining minutes of his life so that he would not become unnerved by the sight of the crowd.

An estimated crowd of 12,000 people - 'almost all', it was reported haughtily, 'without exception, from the lower class of our population' - were prevented from reaching the foot of the scaffold by a phalanx of special constables. But there were no unruly scenes, although the hangman was the target of 'repeated yells of execration'.

(Despite the journalistic jibe at the working classes, it should be noted that Gordon of Craigmyle - 'a most benevolent and kindhearted man' - had a mania for attending executions, and would even go on the fatal platform with the criminal!).

Reverend Strahan read Burnett's dying confession: 'I have confessed my sin that I am to suffer for to man and I hope God will forgive me for all my sins for Christ's sake and your presence gentlemen. I declare there was no one knew of it but myself. I confessed all to Mr Strahan the chaplain. May God be merciful to me, a sinner for Christ's sake. Amen'.

The day before he hanged Burnett wrote a letter to his fellow prisoners urging them to read their Bible and consider its teachings. He also suggested they scrutinize a tract, 'The Sinner's Friend' and a book. 'Clark's Scripture Promises'.

'Think then where you stand my fellow sinners', he wrote. 'Tomorrow is my day - yours may be next'.

His last words on the scaffold were: 'Lord have mercy on my soul'.

Death was instantaneous. His body had hung for less than half-an-hour but this time it was not handed over to the anatomists but buried instead for the first time within the precincts of the East Prison.

Before five months had elapsed it would be joined by the corpse of 22-year-old labourer James Robb, who was tried and found guilty at the Autumn Circuit Court for the murder and rape of a 63-year-old woman in her home at Redhill, Auchterless. William Calcraft travelled from London to hang Robb before a crowd which included many women.

The Autumn Circuit Court of 1849 was a veritable 'Black Kalendar' for Aberdeen, with the judges dealing with cases of murder, rape, pocket picking, counterfeiting and horse theft. A notorious pick-pocket Thomas Kilhoolie got seven years' transportation and his howls and yells on receiving the sentence were heard in Castle Street.

William Skene writing in 'East Neuk Chronicles', ventured as far as the Duke of Gordon statue in Castle Street on the day of Burnett's hanging. His youthful gaze took in the terrible pageant.

He wrote: 'The procession made its appearance through a window in the Town House. The town's officers, to the number of eight or ten, headed by Charlie Dawson, Horne, Mellis, and Leslie, led the van, and then followed the culprit, supported by warders and prison officials. The wretched man wore a black suit and white night-cap, and he was attended by Rev Dr Macintosh, of the East Church.

'As soon as the procession appeared, I fled the scene, and saw no more of James Burnett'.

Chapter Fifteen

Slaughter in Kittybrewster

Airt and pairt in Dauney's Slaughter is an obsolete Aberdeen proverb that can be traced to a dubious story of murder.

Dauney, or Downie, was a tyrannical King's College sacrist, it was said, who died of fright at the hands of students during his mock trial and execution.

So if anything is done, for good or evil, in a company which cannot be found out, then all present are 'art and part of Downie's slaughter'. An old street cry hurled at Aberdeen students was, 'Fa killed Downie?'

The story by Dundee weaver's son Robert Mudie first appeared in 1825, and is completely fictitious.

'Dauney's Howe', a green mound in a hollow 'to the north of Belmont in Kittybrewster', was said to be Downie's grave. A cairn marking the spot was later moved to Tillydrone, where it can still be seen. Downie's Howe vanished in 1926 when the Northern Co-operative Society built its dairy at Berryden.

In October 1852 'Dauney's Howe' was located within yards of a house where one of Aberdeen's most brutal crimes occurred.

But, unlike the Downie legend, there was no mystery.

Widow Ross and her six-year-old grandson were the innocent victims of the 'monster' George Christie, who slaughtered them in her home of Sunnybank, which stood a short distance from the tollbar at Kittybrewster.

A blindfolded Downie died of heart failure when his 'executioner' flicked a wet cloth across the back of his neck.

Christie polished off his victims with an axe.

Christie, who was 51 years old, had served 27 years in the army - 20 of them in India. His career had been far from exemplary, having been reduced from the rank of sergeant. While in civilian life he lost his meagre private's pension when convicted of theft.

Barbara Ross earned her living by cow-feeding and other such tasks. Christie, as fate would have it, thrashed corn in a barn next door to her humble home.

Two days before the murders Christie overheard her say she was selling two of her pigs. No doubt his eyes gleamed at the thought of the money they would fetch. He laid his plans.

On Monday evening, the 4th of October, Christie set off on foot for Kittybrewster, informing an acquaintance in Virginia Street that he had left something behind in the barn. That was around eight.

Mrs Ross and her grandson, John Louden, whose seaman father was away, were together in the house.

At nine, a gardener called McRobbie went down to the barn. Christie had been hired to thrash his corn. McRobbie found the barn door shut. Peering closely through the window of Widow Ross's house he saw the six-foot figure of Christie walking about inside with a lighted candle. Barbara Ross lay slumped on the floor in front of the fireplace.

McRobbie knocked on the door. Christie doused the candle flame before answering. He appeared agitated. Moaning sounds came from within the house.

McRobbie asked for the key to the barn and was handed it. But his suspicions were aroused and he immediately sought the home of another neighbour, Grant. They returned to the widow's house and asked Christie to accompany them to the barn. On the way they inquired about the 'groaning'. McRobbie replied coolly enough: 'The boy had a sair belly'.

The two farmers kept a close watch on Christie as he returned to the widow's house. They were still around when Christie left with a bundle under his arms. He locked the door carefully then walked off, whistling.

The two men summoned the rural policeman, Richardson, who was stationed at Printfield, and he arrived post haste. When they smashed open the door the sight that greeted them was horrific. The room resembled a butcher's shop. The floor was slick with blood and both the old woman and the wee boy had been 'frightfully gashed and mangled' by an axe.

Richardson lost no time in reporting the murders to the Procurator Fiscal in Aberdeen. Then Richardson and Nicol, a night patrolman, went in search of Christie. They were able to trace him through his employer who had hired him to McRobbie.

It was half-past midnight when they found Christie, drunk and confused, with the woman with whom he cohabited in a house in the city's Denburn. They had been supping liquor bought with blood money he had raised by pawning the stolen goods.

The widow's purse, wedding ring, and other articles, including 14 shillings and sixpence in money, were found in his pockets. He was marched off to the lock-up where police noticed the blood stains on his shoes, trousers and shirt.

Christie stood trial on murder charges at the High Court of Justiciary in Edinburgh, two days before Christmas Day 1852. During the trial the prisoner presented a 'dogged, sullen and un-feeling outlook'. Only when the evidence touched on gory details of the murders did Christie draw his breath sharply 'as if sighing inwardly'.

Otherwise he remained perfectly calm and composed during the seven-hour trial, and on receiving the guilty verdict and death sentence.

The Lord Justice Clerk placed the black cap on his head and said: 'In respect of the verdict above recorded, the Lords Justice-Clerk, Lords Cowan and Anderson, discern and adjudge you, the said George Christie, to be carried from the bar of the prison in Edinburgh, and under a sure guard to be transmitted to the prison of Aberdeen, therein to be detained, and fed on bread and water only, till the 13th day of January next, and between 8 and 10 of the forenoon of that day, ordain the said George Christie to be taken out of the said prison to the common place of execution, to be hanged by the neck on a gibbet till you be dead; and ordain your body to be buried within the precincts of the prison; and may God Almighty have mercy upon your soul'.

It was a perfect day for a hanging, unless you were the condemned man.

The man from the 'Aberdeen Herald' left us this colourful description:-

'The morning was intensely cold, the frost being keener than it had been during the season. There was scarcely a breath of wind, and the smoke of the city hung over it like a mortcloth, increasing the darkness by the heavy clouds in the atmosphere'.

Ten thousand pairs of eyes focussed on Christie, whose gait gave a clue to his military background. Scribes noted there were fewer females than usual among the spectators, who were prevented from reaching the gallows by a double barricade.

Few present looked on Christie with any pity.

Journalist William Carnie, who took down the felon's dying

94

words for posterity, recalled years later: 'Christie had few sympathisers. The Kittybrewester murder of an old woman and a young child was unprovoked, a cruel deed!'

Christie kept his composure. But it was noted he seemed 'much emaciated' since his trial. 'His whole person appearing to be shrunk, but his mind was evidently collected, and even composed, and his bearing was respectful and resigned'.

The doomed man spent a sleepless night, choosing to pace the floor of his cell like a caged animal while trying to find solace in the Bible.

He managed to eat a light breakfast and just after eight the bearded figure of William Calcraft, the celebrated public hangman, appeared in his cell. Calcraft, an executioner since 1829, was paid a guinea a week by the City of London and a guinea for every execution in the capital. He held office as public executioner for a longer period than any other man - 45 years.

Calcraft pinioned his arms and at 8.15am Christie began his last walk.

The Provost asked him if he had anything to say before going to the scaffold and he replied firmly: 'No-nothing'.

A low murmur rose from the throats of the spectators who pressed in on the scaffold. In later times a venerable octogenarian who witnessed public hangings in Aberdeen would recall: 'You couldna' get a richt sicht o' him unless you was close in by'.

On the drop Calcraft asked the condemned man to signal with the white napkin when ready.

Christie, showing great stoicism, asked Calcraft: *'Are you ready?'*, Calcraft replied 'yes' and Christie spoke for the last time: 'Now gentlemen. I'm quite ready'.

He then, with deliberate movement of his hand, threw down the napkin. He died with little struggling and apparent suffering.

But as the drop fell with a clatter a woman, perhaps Christie's paramour, emitted a wild, piercing shriek.

Tyrie Church, Aberdeenshire, where Boyndlie murderer James
Burnett and his intended bride set tongues wagging in 1848.

ONE PENNY Only

Catherine Humphrey, the last woman to hang in Aberdeen, kept
a public house in the notorious 'Bool Road', later Albion Street.
(Author's Collection).

London-based executioner William Calcraft was hired to hang three murderers in Aberdeen, including James Booth, the last person to be publicly hanged in the city.
(From Laurence's 'A History of Capital Punishment').

Kirktown of St Fergus, looking along Netherhill Road. Farmer McDonald's corpse was found in a field somewhere to the left.

Chapter Sixteen

The St Fergus Mystery

At St Fergus, the pancake-flat landscape, dominated by the silvery complex and flare stack of Europe's biggest gas terminal, marches into the North Sea.

To the south, beyond Peterhead, soars another 20th century landmark - the muckle tower of Boddam power station.

Helicopters clatter overhead, bound for Aberdeen Airport, or an offshore oil rig. The idea of a flying machine would have been beyond the wildest imagination of the good people who sleep forever in older graves beside the ruined kirk, next to the fertile fields and sand dunes.

On the landward edge of the road that links Peterhead, four miles to the south, and Fraserburgh, the hamlet of Kirktown of St Fergus is tucked behind the new village.

Kirktown hasn't changed much with the passage of time. It comprises of a single street of cottages, running east to west, with a post office and a Victorian church. Yes, time seems to have stood still.

But the St Fergus mystery is all but forgotten.

On a rainy November evening in 1853 a young widower, farmer William McDonald, set off from his widowed mother's home to walk the two miles to Kirktown of St Fergus, where he had a six o'clock appointment with his good friend, the village doctor.

McDonald, hale and hearty and engaged to be married, next appeared around seven in the shop of James Smith, junior, the local cartwright, where he inquired about a pair of haims (harness accoutrements), which he had ordered, a grub-harrow for neeps and some paling for the farm.

That evening - Saturday the 19th - McDonald was in his usual health and spirits, and full of banter. At around half-past seven he left the shop with the parting remark: 'It's getting late. I've need to be away'.

He was never seen alive again.

After an anxious night waiting for William's return to the family's small farm at Burnside, north-west of Kirktown, his young brother Robert went out to search for him.

The next morning, Sunday, the 20th, he found his brother's body in a ditch next to a field owned by McDonald's friend, Dr William Smith, and 500 yards from the doctor's home. The body lay in an inch of water at the bottom of the ditch. There was a bullet hole in the right cheek and the deceased's face was blackened with gunpowder. A pistol was lying on the ground about four feet from the corpse's head.

A horrified Robert ran to fetch Dr Smith. He was out, so the boy left a message with his wife before returning to the death scene.

Shortly afterwards Dr Smith and a farmer James Pirie found Robert crying over his brother's body. 'God preserve us', exclaimed the doctor. He picked up the pistol and said: 'That's the thing that's done it', suggesting suicide.

When the body was searched there was no trace of gunpowder or shot and the pockets of McDonald's jacket were too small to conceal a pistol.

Dr Smith, who had been the family doctor for the past eight years, broke the tragic news to widow McDonald. He told the distraught woman her son 'had done it himself', and that he had most probably 'suffocated or drowned'.

But Mrs McDonald refused to believe her son had taken his own life. He had never owned a pistol. Mrs McDonald suspected foul play and the doctor warned her 'that she would get into trouble for the way she was speaking'.

She asked Dr Smith if William had kept his appointment with him the previous evening but he denied there was any arrangement between them to meet that night. It transpired they had met regularly for a month before the fatal shooting.

Dr Smith filled out the death certificate, inferring the shooting was 'not likely to have been done by any other than the deceased'. He took charge of McDonald's funeral arrangements and remarked to widow McDonald: 'If Boyd heard what had happened, he would be out', meaning the Procurator Fiscal would come from Peterhead to investigate the death.

On the Monday forenoon, two days before the funeral, the Fiscal did arrive in the village. He asked two doctors - Comrie and Gordon - to examine the locus and carry out a post mortem examination. The post mortem showed death had been instantane-

-ous - a bullet lodged in the brain, fired from a distance between three to 13 inches from the head. The doctors could only account for the position of the body if McDonald had shot himself sitting or lying in the ditch, or had been placed in it by another person.

As a result of their findings Dr Smith was arrested on a charge of murder the following day and taken to Peterhead.

The case should have been heard at the High Court of Justiciary in Edinburgh on Monday, March 13, 1854, but a juryman took ill and the diet was continued until Wednesday, April 12, with Lord Justice Clerk Hope and Lords Cowan and Handyside on the bench. The courtroom, noted a reporter, was 'filled by a most respectable audience, including a considerable number of ladies'.

(Lord Hope and Dr Smith's defence counsel would later preside at the trial of Madeleine Smith).

The dilemma that faced the jury - was McDonald shot dead by a trusted friend - or did he commit suicide?

On the second day of the trial it was revealed that the life of William McDonald had been insured with three separate insurance companies - the Northern, Caledonian and Scottish Mutual - for the grand total of £2,000, in favour of Dr William Smith.

McDonald had gone along with the doctor, believing money might be borrowed against the policies. When an insurance agent expressed astonishment at McDonald's ignorance and indifference he replied: 'The doctor's a fine chiel, and I have always done as he bade me do'.

The prosecution proved that the accused owned two pistols. The St Fergus blacksmith William Murison had repaired the trigger of a pistol, the very weapon produced in court.

The court heard how Dr Smith had bought a few ounces of gunpowder from a St Fergus merchant Alexander McLeod on the day of the shooting. He told McLeod he needed the gunpowder to make up ointment for a girl patient. McLeod told the court he was well acquainted with the deceased and he had never sold him gunpowder before.

There was a macabre touch. Dr Smith purchased McDonald's shroud from McLeod (he ordered the coffin from the village cartwright) and recalled an earlier conversation when the doctor thought the shot had only wounded McDonald and 'that it was partly a case of drowning'.

A claim by Dr Smith that there had been a 'hurry' - disagreement - in the McDonald family, which had preyed on the deceased's mind, was refuted by the local minister, McDonald's mother and his fiancee, Mary Slessor.

Dr Smith's defence weighed heavily upon alibi, and there was much said about his whereabouts at the time of the shooting, which took place around 7.35pm. The bellman had left his home to ring the nightly eight o'clock curfew when he saw a flash to the south-west and heard the crack of a pistol.

Dr Smith did not meet McDonald at six. He was at the manse, treating a sick servant. He later called on three other homes in the village.

At the time of the shooting the doctor declared he was visiting a patient, Isabella Anderson. On arriving at her home he made great play of drawing her attention to the time - twenty five minutes to eight. She did not tell him the clock was then quarter of an hour slow, and the actual time of his visit was ten minutes to eight.

So there was a gap of between 15 minutes which the good doctor could not account for.

There was a mild sensation in court when Adam Gray, the brother of the Provost of Peterhead, appeared as the last witness in the case.

He claimed he had sold a pistol to William McDonald who said he wanted to 'frighten rooks from the crops'. Gray, who was a friend of Dr Smith, believed it to be the same pistol found beside the deceased's body. In court he produced a jotter recording the transaction.

After retiring for 10 minutes the jury brought in a verdict of 'not proven' but by a majority only. The Lord Justice Clerk, in summing up, said that although the whole case was surrounded with suspicion and with difficulties, the evidence had failed to connect the shooting with the prisoner at the bar.

Lord Hope asked the jury - 'Perhaps it is right that I should just ask you, in such a case as this, whether the difference of opinion was as to 'Not Proven' or 'Not Guilty'?'. The jury foreman gave the unexpected reply - 'Our opinion was between 'Guilty' and 'Not Proven', my Lord'.

A sound like escaping gas greeted the verdict. As Dr Smith left the bar he was taken aside for his own protection, an act which touched off an even louder storm of hissing from the crowded benches. There was a delay before Dr Smith stepped into the Auld

Reekie night to be reunited with his wife and family. After a week-end in Edinburgh they returned to Aberdeen by steamer, thence by carriage to St Fergus.

News of the verdict was greeted with shocked disbelief in Buchan, and there was criticism of the manner in which the trial was conducted. Newspapers ran special editions, and the war in the Crimea took a back seat.

Dr Smith? Despite his acquittal he was never able to collect payment for the policies of insurance. Civil actions were raised by his lawyer, but the insurance companies fought them vigorously, and the policies lapsed.

Criminal history, too, repeats itself. Forty years later a similar mystery shooting took place at Ardlamont House on the Kyles of Bute, with a similar outcome.

Chapter Seventeen

The Last Drop

In 1857, the year of the Indian Mutiny and the sensational Madeleine Smith murder trial, the peace and tranquillity of an Aberdeenshire market town was disrupted by two major events. One triumphant, the other tragic.

The tragedy in Oldmeldrum centred on a tottering tenement in Weavery Lane where dreams of health, wealth and happiness were hawked.

A labourer's wife, Jean Barclay, earned extra coppers foretelling the future in the low-roofed home that also served as her crockery shop.

She and a neighbourly married daughter Mary, a stout, ruddy complexioned mother of two, had the knack of telling fortunes by reading tea leaves, palms and by the turn of the playing card. Sometimes these sessions spilled over to the Sabbath.

Neither woman could imagine what fate had in store for them.

Nemesis came in the shape of Mary's 37-year-old husband, John Booth, a dark-browed man, small in stature, but with a 'piercing quick eye' and a taste for liquor.

Their stormy marriage was blighted with continual brawling with his wife and her 60-year-old mother. The drink-inflamed rows were blamed on everything from his wife's infidelity to telling fortunes on a Sunday.

Taunts by fellow hawkers about Mary's unfaithfulness drove Booth to the edge of madness.

After peering thunderstruck through a window at Mary making love to a man in their bed he attempted suicide.

Inflamed with booze he swallowed a bottle of poison before the eyes of the two women and sobbed: 'See I'll not trouble you no more'. But he survived.

Booth would later claim he had spied on his mother-in-law in bed with a married man but his accusations were greeted with the cry of 'liar, liar' by the old woman and her frail, 70-year-old husband, James.

Booth had been drinking with his cronies at Oldmeldrum on the evening of Tuesday, July 21. 1857, when a row flared over the subject of his wife's unfaithfulness. Thoughts of travelling with his box of wares to the horse fair at Aikey Brae the next day were forgotten in the heat of the moment.

He rushed home and set about Mary with his 'deer knife', a large, spring-backed clasp knife, but was either too drunk or too slow for she managed to escape. She dashed from her bed in her night attire and made it into the street, blood oozing from a wound.

Jean Barclay was not so lucky. She and her husband were in bed when Mary wakened them by hammering on the door of the shuttered house. She had barely gasped out her story when Booth, brandishing the knife, burst into the room on the ground floor of the mean dwelling.

Jean, armed with roller, attempted to block Booth's wild charge. She stood between him and her daughter and became the target of his knife thrusts. He stabbed her seven or eight times between the neck and lower ribs, but the fatal blow went straight to the heart. 'Mary', she shouted, 'rin for yer life, this man has murdered me!'

The Booth's only son, James, who was about nine years old, watched the horrible scene as he stood terrified on a chair. At the Circuit Court trial in Aberdeen in September he was too young to take the oath but he told the Lord Justice Clerk Hope and Lord Deas: 'I've been taught to read the Bible and my Testament and I know I will be punished by God if I do wrong, and I'm bound to tell the truth'.

What he saw was his drunken father struggle with his grandfather and the old man deal Booth a blow on the head with a shovel. 'I ran from the house', said the boy, shouting 'Grannie is dead!'

The blood-stained knife lay at the doorway of the murder house, with Booth inside. He was arrested by the local policeman and because Oldmeldrum had no lock-up, he spent the night in chains, fettered at the parlour fireside in the local Carle's Inn, now Morris's Hotel. It must have been hell on earth for Booth. I wonder if the mine host gave him a dram to steady his nerves?

Newshounds were quick off the mark. When a scribe reached the scene of the tragedy they found old Barclay wandering the lanes near his home 'with his head bent upon his breast and his hands thrust far into his trouser pockets looking like one very cold and dreary though the sun shone and warmly'.

Inside the gloomy dwelling, at the back of the rude counter of the small shop, lay the body of Jean Barclay, 'clothed and bloody as she had fallen with a face as white as the driven snow'.

Aberdeen journalist and psalmodist William Carnie (1824-1908), a shorthand wizard who sharpened his skills by taking verbatim notes of his minister's sermons, much to the reverend gentleman's chagrin, left us a poignant description of the scene of the crime.

'According to popular rumour', he wrote, 'the stabbed woman was the real cause of all the family unhappiness. But the deed was done, and when a couple of hours after the blows had been struck I entered the very humble dwelling situated in a back lane of the village, a little caged bird was singing above the dead woman, singing as blithely as if it had been its native bush'.

Young James Booth, whose court ordeal had yet to come, and his three-year-old sister cowered on a straw-filled sack, while their mother, stunned into silence by the murder, sat with her back to the front door 'never looking at who passed in or out'.

Almost quarter-a-century after the murder George Webster, the Sheriff and Criminal Officer at Oldmeldrum - 'my tongue runs freest i' the native Doric' - recalled: 'Booth made nae attempt till escape, but loot the constable lay han's on him at ance - I cudna be gotten at the instant. Booth was perfectly frantic at the time against baith his wife an's mither-in-law, and said he was sorry he hedna been able to punish the wife as she deserv't - she got only a bit cut aboot the fingers.

'Hoosomever, fan the hue an' cry got up, as I was sayin', I got notice in five minutes or so. Gars them tak' Booth to Carle's Inn, an' rins for Dr Ingram at ance. But doctors war o' nae use as far's the injur't 'oman was concern't - she was gone. There was nae licht i' the hoose faur the fray happen't, an' I ran hame an' got a can'le, an' syne aifter search fan the knife - a spring-backit ane, wi' a deer horn han'le. I seals it up, an' labels 't of coorse. An' a' this bein' owre I gets a gig an' horse, an' sets aff for Aberdeen at the clean-ever-leavin' to inform the Fiscal an' Sheriff'.

The next day Webster escorted Booth into Aberdeen. A great mob waited for them to alight from the train at Waterloo Station, down by the quay, but Webster 'manag't to dodge them, an' wan up b' the Barracks wi' my prisoner, an' across to the jail wi' little or nae notice'. Booth pleaded guilty to culpable homicide but his plea was not accepted by the Crown.

In summing up Lord Hope told the jury it was true there had been no proven enmity on the part of the prisoner toward the deceased - but that was not necessary to form a case of murder. His Lordship, after pointing out that a person might deprive another of life by a single stroke of a knife without any evil intent, repeated, that if the jury found any alleviating circumstances in the case they would return a verdict accordingly. If they thought it was a case to which the plea of culpable homicide did not apply, they would return a verdict of murder.

It took the jury 40 minutes to reach a verdict - guilty of murder.

Just as the Lord Justice Clerk was about to pronounce doom, Booth, amid considerable excitement from the spectators in court, waved his hand and said: 'Please your worship, I have a word to say if you will permit me'.

He was allowed to continue. Booth, pointing dramatically heavenwards, said solemnly: 'I shall speak the truth as I shall answer to God'.

Tension gripped the courtroom as Booth told of his wife's infidelity and how he had played Peeping Tom - watching her have 'connection' with a man in bed at their home. There was another witness to the affair - a gardener friend, William Saunders, who had asked Booth: 'Can you do nothing? Can you stand that?'

Booth told how he had bought sixpenny worth of poison and 'teemed' a draught sufficient to kill a man, in front of Mary and her mother. But because he had been drinking booze he turned violently sick, and lived.

'I might have said more but I will conclude with that!' he told a stunned court.

At the conclusion of this strange statement, the Lord Justice Clerk placed the black cap on his head and sent Booth to the gallows - the execution fixed between eight and ten on the morning of Wednesday, October 21.

Booth was no ignorant brute, and sympathy went out to him from all quarters. Efforts were being made behind the scenes by influential gentlemen in Aberdeen to save his neck.

Among his visitors to the condemned cell in the East Prison were his 35-year-old wife Mary, who was born in Daviot, their two youngsters, and his father-in-law, for whom he had liking, despite what had gone before. These trysts were described as 'affectionate and touching' and their real purpose would be revealed on the scaffold.

Oldmeldrum was still reeling from the shock of the murder when it heard joyous news. It was to receive Royal visitors.

Queen Victoria and Prince Albert, with members of their family, would pass through the burgh at the end of their annual pilgrimage to Balmoral. The royals would spend the night at Haddo House, Lord Aberdeen's retreat, before boarding the London train in Aberdeen the following day.

The royal procession would travel from Balmoral to Haddo House, via Ballater, Tarland, Craigievar, Alford, Inverurie and Oldmeldrum.

The October day chosen for the glorious event fell exactly a week before Booth was due to hang.

Oldmeldrum was agog. Sixty special constables, with white gloves and batons, controlled the huge crowds lining the streets. Four elegant arches decorated the route through the town, the best one erected by Sheriff Officer George Webster, who had 'borrow't aboot twa hunner an' fifty flags, an' hed the village flaggit't ye saw never the like i' yer born days'. Before breakfast Mr Webster, in 'foul sark', and two carpenters nailed up the flags. An hour or so later he was greeting the Fiscal and other officials from Aberdeen in his 'black breeks, wi' a gold lace band roun' my hat' and rosettes given by local ladies.

The Queen was enthralled by the welcome and ordered the royal coach to drive slowly through the town. As the last carriage passed Captain Ramsay of Barra, at the gates of Meldrum House, the town celebrated in style. A band from Aberdeen serenaded the populace as invited guests drifted to the town hall to drink toasts and make speeches. The great day was rounded off with a spectacular fireworks display.

The 'Aberdeen Herald' carried a highly descriptive article on the royal cavalcade through the country, and subsequent junket at Haddo, but a short paragraph at the end of the report had no doubt sobered readers.

It read: 'Up to the moment we write, we regret much to say that there does not appear to be the slightest chance of a reprieve for poor John Booth, whose execution remains for Wednesday first'.

Booth, fed on a diet of bread and water since the end of his trial, managed to snatch some sleep in the death cell. He rose between three and four on the morning of his execution. The day before he dictated and signed his dying confession.

107

As he washed and dressed he could hear the thump of the carpenters' hammers as they built his gallows, but he made no comment. After prayers with the prison chaplain, Reverend Baxter, and Reverend Land, of the East Church, he breakfasted at 6.30am.

Just before eight a powerful-looking man with flowing white hair and beard to match entered Booth's cell.

The man in black was William Calcraft, the hangman. Booth guessed the stranger's identity and insisted they shook hands. Calcraft, a kind -hearted man who was fond of children and pets, obliged. He never refused a condemned man.

Oldmeldrum's lawman, George Webster, wrote in his colourful memoirs: 'Calcraft was an object of strong interest with the crowd at this moment, but by no means visible. The grim artist had come to Aberdeen on the previous Saturday to make his preparations and survey the situation; but though some had seen a grey-headed man, with thickish shoulders and heavy step walking here and there, cane in hand, he had been disappointingly rare and vague in his appearances before the curious public'.

Booth had his arms pinioned, perhaps in the act of shaking hands. He was taken to the scaffold by a passage from the East Prison. The Lord Provost and magistrates watched the prisoner come up the passage steps in the old courthouse with a 'light, firm step without the least degree of swagger'.

Booth bowed respectfully to the Lord Provost, who asked if he had any last wish and whether or not he had a statement. 'I have given something to Mr Baxter, which he will show you', replied Booth. When Booth said he would address the crowd the Provost suggested he made it short, for many reasons.

Booth walked directly to the scaffold from a window on the first floor of the old burgh courtroom. According to the time-honoured custom, the window had been taken out and masonry below the sill removed to floor level, thus making a doorway onto the scaffold.

A death-like hush fell on the 2,000 spectators as Booth spoke in an attempt to make amends by clearing the names of his wife and family.

'My friends,' he told them, 'you all know what the occasion is for me being here. It is sin. Sin is the greatest cause of my downfall'. He went on: 'I said a few words in court about my wife and my people, which I hope in your presence now you will omit; as what will a man not say to try and save his life?'

The ubiquitous William Carnie stood at Booth's elbow to record the fateful words.

He wrote in his bulky memoirs years later: 'For the second time the gruesome task of standing beside the hangman fell to me, and there in view of the spectators, I took his dying utterances. They were, mercifully, the 'last words' ever spoken publicly from the gallows in our good town.

'There were many thought poor John Booth might have been spared.'

The crowd greeted the end of Booth's confession with a single word: 'Amen!'

Calcraft positioned Booth on the drop. When he fitted the noose around the condemned man's neck a scornful cry of 'Ah!' rose from spectators. Booth seemed as calm as his executioner, noted for his stoicism. The hangman pulled the white stocking over Booth's face. Booth muttered a short prayer, gave the signal, and 'the bolt was withdrawn'. After a few convulsive struggles John Booth, was dead.

Oldmeldrum's George Webster did not attend the execution. But a friend who did go later wrote of his horror at seeing 'a good many young men and women, even boys and girls, in the crowd. Perhaps most revolting of all, mothers with babies in arms and actually pressing against the fence with towsy bare heads, and glancing eagerly up at the grim apparatus of death as they volubly discussed the points of the coming situation'.

Of the hanging itself Webster's acquaintance commented:

'Booth stepped onto the block, and it was then that the crowd, for the first time, fairly got sight of Calcraft as he adjusted his gear, when a savage hiss greeted him. At this significant demonstration the executioner visibly cowered; and from the unenviable point of vantage at Booth's right hand on the scaffold, one could plainly perceive that, despite the dull phlegmatic contour of the official face, and the heavy under jaw, the man at the heart of him was a coward.

'Calcraft pulled the white cap over Booth's face, finally adjusted the rope; for a few seconds his lips could be seen under the cap moving energetically in prayer. Then - the handkerchief falls from his hand, the bolts shoots back with a stiff creak; a dull thud is heard - simply that - as the poor wretch falls, half out of sight of the crowd; the head turns to one side; a few convulsive struggles can be seen; and so is finished a scene such as one fervently desires

109

never to witness the like of again'.

His body hung for 20 minutes before it was removed and buried in the precincts of the East Prison, where three other killers lay - the Boyndlie poisoner James Burnett, James Robb, murderer and rapist, and George Christie, the Kittybrewster murderer.

Booth's body was barely cold in his grave when hawkers of literature were selling lurid versions of the murder and trashy confessions, complete with hideous illustrations. More discerning readers would wait for the local papers.

In his official statement Booth again stressed the folly of his ways and the innocence of his family.

This is what he said: 'The statement which I made in court, at my trial, has given me, and gives me still, the utmost uneasiness and pain, for what will a man not say and do for his life? And I implore, in the near prospect of death and eternity, that sad speech will be forgotten, and never remembered against my dear wife and children. And, further it is my anxious desire that the black deed of which I am guilty, and for which I am to suffer, will never operate against the interests of my dear wife and children. I do from my heart implore my dear wife to forgive me for whatever I've said or done that has wronged her and I earnestly pray that God may be gracious onto her and the children. Bless them'.

What other thoughts passed through Booth's head as he stood on the drop?

He was but a short distance from his birthplace. He was born in a house in Shore Lane, off the Shiprow, in 1820. Booth's mother was banished from Aberdeen for some unknown crime. The town hanged her son.

Booth would never know of his niche in local history.

He was the last person to be hanged in public in Aberdeen - and the last to be executed in the city during the last century. Indeed it was to be 106 years before anyone else died on the scaffold in Aberdeen - Henry Burnett, the last man to hang in Scotland.

By a quirk of fate Calcraft had not seen the last of the Aberdeen gallows.

Twice in 1866 Aberdeen's municipal gallows was loaned to two Scottish towns which did not own such things.

In January, a Stonehaven seaman, Andrew Brown, who murdered his skipper at sea with an axe, was hanged in Montrose. Sentence had been delayed at the Edinburgh High Court because of the difficulty of finding a venue for his execution - in Kincardineshire or Forfarshire. Calcraft required a strong police escort to the railway station afterwards. In May, he hanged poacher Joe Bell outside Perth Jail for the shotgun murder of a baker's vanman near Vicars Bridge, Blairingone, Perthshire. The motive: robbery.

When Calcraft retired in 1874 the City of London gave the famous executioner a pension of 25 shillings a week for life.

Mary Booth re-married.

Chapter Eighteen

To Catch a Thief

George Webster was the law in town, and surrounding coun-tryside. He toted a pistol, hunted criminals on horse-back and sometimes travelled hundreds of miles by stagecoach to get his man. And he would boast: 'That's the hand that's grippet seven murderers!'

But 'Geordie' Webster was no Wild West lawman. He was a Sheriff and Criminal Officer, one of a scattered band who kept law and order in rural Scotland before a regular police force.

Before the end of the 19th century Sheriff Watson of Aberdeen wrote: 'The preservation of the peace of the country was entrusted to a few sheriffs-officers, distributed here and there among the large villages; and from 1832 to 1840, nearly the whole criminal work of the large county of Aberdeen was done, and done in a most efficient manner, by George Webster, in Old Meldrum, who apprehended most of the murderers, housebreakers, and thieves, then more numerous than they are now'.

Geordie loved that. 'No certificate cud weel come ootwith o' that, lat me tell you', he preened. He was never happier unless he got a felon under lock and key in Aberdeen, or, as he described it, 'pitten safe aneth the weather cock'.

Geordie was based in Oldmeldrum. 'A place of considerable importance', he wrote in his memoirs. 'Mair sae nor Inverurie? Ay, I sud think sae; Inverurie, royal burgh that it is, an' for a' its upsettin' noo-a-days, was a mere squattery o' thacket hoosies a hun'er years ago, fan Meldrum was a sturrin' place wi' a weekly market'.

Geordie Webster was born in Oldmeldrum on June 4, 1801. After schooling he worked as a groom for Sir John Forbes of Fintray, who recommended him for the 'criminal bizness', and in 1832 he gained his commission as a Criminal Officer. King William IV was on the throne.

On New Year's Day 1833 the new lawman was involved in a thrilling chase on horse-back. He was on the trail of a housebreaker, fleeing south with his booty. The pursuit began in Pitcaple and ended beyond Inverurie. During the night-long chase, in which hunter and hunted crossed and recrossed the River Urie, they exchanged fire. At Kintore the villain was finally overpowered by locals while Geordie 'wus in at the death in a jiffey' and 'a pair o' mittens clappit on wi' little mair adee'.

Geordie's duties included attending fairs and markets, a magnet for all sorts of criminals, ranging from pick-pockets to horse thieves. He and a colleague would wear red coats, their badge of authority, discreetly hidden under jackets until the moment of truth.

Geordie was handy with his fists in a tight situation, but could also give Sherlock Holmes a run for his money. In May 1837 he snared a thief by footprints in the snow. He took an impression of the prints on a piece of paper and compared them with the soles of boots worn by a cattle-dealer at Huntly market. They matched and the thief was transported for seven years. The 'prent o' the muckle tackettie shee sole' in a blacksmith's yard helped nail Sawney Lindsay, and old smuggler - 'a coorse blackguard' according to Geordie - who has been stealing bees. Geordie made the arrest in the Small Debt Court in Aberdeen.

Geordie made a number of unusual and daring arrests during his 46 years' service.

In July 1838 he was enjoying himself right fine at the Reform Ball in Inverurie, when, still in Highland dress, he was summoned to investigate a theft at Fyvie Castle.

A butler John Watson had reported the theft of a great quantity of linen and garments.

Geordie suspected a former servant Jane Ritchie, who had sent a heavy trunk by carrier to Oldmeldrum. Geordie forced open the trunk and found it packed with the stolen goods and pawnbroker's tickets. He found more goods in William Ruddiman's shop in the Green in Aberdeen. Geordie arrested Ritchie on her wedding day, with her 'deckit up like a duchess'. The bride fainted and had to be revived with a splash of water. 'Hoot, hoot', says I, 'tak' care an' nae weet 'er owre sair, for though I'm takin' 'er awa' fae the bridegreem, I'm takin' 'er to Aiberdeen in a braw cairriage'.

Geordie then relieved the blacksmith bridegroom of 'a deev'lish ill wife'. It seems Ritchie, who had been stealing from other big houses where she had worked, had a child by the groom in jail in Aberdeen. Commented Geordie: 'It was a laddie, an' of coorse he grew up a freeman o' the toon, bein' born i' the jail'.

Ritchie was eventually sent to Botany Bay.

In the spring of 1841 Geordie disguised himself as an old woman to nab poacher John Rose in the Earl of Kintore's woods at Ley Lodge. In borrowed garments he crept up on Rose as he lifted the snares. 'Lord preserve's!', cried Rose. 'Aw thocht it was an aul' wife!' Replied Geordie: 'Ay, ay; and' sae I am - a gey queer aul' wife, tee. However, pack ye up your traps an' come along, laddie'. Rose had time to recover from his surprise arrest in the Aberdeen Bridewell.

There was the time he tracked a thieving pair of tinkers - 'roch oonchristian tykes' - from the Bridge of Alford to a sea cave at Troup Head, near Gardenstown, There, with the aid of half-a-dozen farm servants, wielding pitch forks and other weapons, Geordie 'slippit into the cave canny aneuch, an' got half-a dizzen o' the tribe an' mair, wives an' bairns an' a', lyin' there deid drunk or sleepin', an' the sea washin' to the door o' their hoose. We hed them han'-cuff't ere they hardly got their een apen't, so there was nae difficulty in managing them'.

The two robbers, Jock and Geordie Williamson, were banished.

No crime was too big or too small for our Geordie. While beadle at Oldmeldrum kirk he investigated the case of the vanishing collection! It happened three Sundays on the trot. Suspicion fell on Jeems Crichton, an elder, who went round with the collection plate. 'The minister an' the session wus in a maze aboot it', recalled Geordie.

Geordie kept watch from outside the kirk during a service and caught the thief red-handed. He was a young lad, the 'nickum Farquhar', and , despite the minister's protests, Geordie marched the offender off to jail in Aberdeen!

In the early part of his career he investigated a break-in at Sandy Bothwell's house in Kirk Street, Oldmeldrum, and the theft of a watch at George Hunter's farm at Mill of Easterton.

The thief was a farm labourer William Simpson, whom Geordie found hiding under the 'cauff bed' at his home, with his 'wife an' 's faimily a' lyin' o' the tap the bed abeen 'im'. Simpson got seven years - 'an deet afore his sentence was oot'.

George Webster travelled near and far to track down criminals.

If he was not on horseback or driving a gig, he would journey by stagecoach. *Tally-ho, Earl of Fife, Lord Forbes* or the *Union*, were some of the names of these coaches.

114

In April 1835 he went in search of George Walker, former guard of the Star coach, which plied between Aberdeen and Elgin. Walker, who had 'gane the black gate wi' drink', stole £91 from a Huntly merchant at Sangster's Inn, Newmachar.

Geordie searched all night long for Walker but he had got clean away. As Geordie pointed out it could prove difficult catching a criminal who had a day or two's head start. 'Ye hed to set a' yer wits at wark than to get tracks o' 'im. It wasna - Warn Edinboro', Dundee or Glaisca by telegraph, an' speer at the poleece richt an' left 'Have ye seen 'im? - five fit ten, licht hair, curled whiskers, an' a side-lang leuk - dressed in grey tweed fan last seen'. Na, na - jist a blin' glamp; an' dash awa' upo' your ain skeel in search o' yer prisoner, man or 'oman. Letter reetin' an' wytein' for days for an answer did ye little gweed'.

By a stroke of luck the following spring, Geordie was returning from Liverpool on criminal work when the Union coach stopped at Haddington. After a dram with the local police superintendent he was invited to cast an eye over the prisoners - and in one cell he confronted the fugitive Walker, in jail for debt. 'Hilloa, Geordie, 'quo I; 'a gyuan fit's aye gettin', ye see'. Ye sud' a seen foo bumbaiz't the beggar luikit fan he saw me though'. Walker was taken north for questioning and then returned to Edinburgh where he was eventually banished by the Justiciary Court.

Geordie showed the same true grit on other occasions.

In July 1843 he arrested a forger, James Duncan, at Portsoy. On the return trip as he came 'rattlin' alang on the tap o' the Earl of Fife coach wi' my prisoner', Duncan complained his handcuffs were chaffing his wrists.

Geordie had no sooner removed the cuffs than his prisoner made a break for freedom by leaping from the coach which was 'gaen at ten mile i' the 'oor'. The coach halted and, with the help of a group of students, baying like a pack of fox hounds, Geordie ran Duncan to earth. For the rest of the journey to Meldrum the prisoner wore handcuffs and leg irons. Geordie had covered no less than 122 miles on the case.

At the end of the previous year he had gone in search of a man called Nicol - 'to Edinburgh, to Glasgow, to Greenock an' back, pairt railway, pairt coach, occupied one week, 400 miles in all'. Nicol eluded him, but was outlawed at the next Circuit Court.

Geordie Webster risked life and limb.

In 1836 he was badly hurt while making a difficult arrest at a slate quarry at Tillymorgan. Murdoch Finlayson, a 'great robust young deevle', hurled him down a slope when he tried to arrest him on an assault charge. Despite a serious head injury he managed to overpower the man with the help of some quarrymen and rope him to a cart. In court the next day Sheriff Watson eyed the arresting officer's bandaged head and said: 'Oh, Geordie, ye've been at the wars, have ye?' Geordie replied: 'Oh, yes, sir. I've been at the wars, an' bear the marks upo' me'.

Oldmeldrum's Criminal Officer of the 'old school' injured his ribs when caught up in an 'unholy row' at Culsalmond Church. It was the time of the Disruption, when 451 ministers of the Church of Scotland and almost a third of the membership left the Established Church on the principle of spiritual independence from the State to form the Free Kirk.

At stake was the right of the congregation to 'call' its own minister without accepting one through patronage. A crowd of a thousand and more beseiged the church to prevent the new minister 'settled'. Geordie was in the thick of things, along with other Sheriff Officers and the police. 'But a' the officers an' police there cudna stem ae grain; an' I naitrally steed a peer chance, for I was yarkit in aside the door an' knockit doon. An' I suppose fifty o' them gaed richt owre me we' their feet, the haethens.'

Geordie suffered broken ribs and had to be carried to the manse and put to bed. That night he went home in Sheriff Murray's carriage.

Geordie Webster religiously kept a note of his arrests, and expenses, in a little 'beuk'. Here is a glimpse of a few entries from one of his books. His pawky humour shines throughout!

'The simmer o' 1841 was occupiet wi' fat ye mith ca' miscellaneous cases... July 1st, apprehendin' ane James Wishart for forgery; syne at the middle o' the same month awa to Laurencekirk, Brechin, Arbroath, Dundee an' Glasgow aifter anither forger; an' on the 24th doon to Banff for George Chalmers, 't hed been flunky at Meldrum Hoose. Oh, he was chairg't wi' theft, an' got sixty days in jail. On August 10th, apprehendin' Alexander Munro, carter, Cotton, for assault on Charles McCrae; that was Charles the vinter in Meldrum ye ken. He kicket up a great row, an' brak' Charles' windows an' the vera door, the great haethen. He was in drink of coorse; but he got sixty days to sober upon 't ony wye. On the 22nd October, I was o' the hunt to Stanehive, the fisherton o' Downies, an' Stripeside, Fetteresso, aifter Catherine Thain, alias

Ann Robertson, an' I got her in Widow Falconer's there. It was a case of theft at Forres, an' she got thirty days.'

'On the 6th and 7th November, ye'll see I was aifter Joseph Tohetto, for brakin' into the shop o' James Robertson, wricht, Craigdam, an' stealin' a quantity o' tools. I huntit up the tools, some o' them buriet i' the fields, an' Joseph got sixty days private lodgin's in Aberdeen. A curious case o' malicious mischief cam' up on the 8th, fan I hed to fae to Morayfield, Auchterless, an' mak' inquiries against Alexander Forbes, farm-servan' there, an' ither twa, Alexander Grant an' James Grieve, a' three o' them reckless young scamps, for dingin' doon several ruckies belongin' till a man Adam Chapman, a crafter at Redhill o' Auchterless. An' forbye that, they tied Chapman himsel' wi' a rope that he cudna win ott. 'Arcadian innocence an' simplicity', said ye, Sir? I ken naething aboot Arcadian nor Kirkcaldian innocence; but that was a piece o' curs't mischief ony wye; an' they paid for 't wi' sixty days i' the jail, an' sair't them right tee, I tell ye'!

In 1880, Geordie wrote somewhat scornfully of the contemporary force:

'Fat? There's nae ae vagabon' the day, I tell ye, faur there was a dizzeen - ay a score - fan I began; and ye've seyventy or auchty police i' the Coonty stappin' roon' like as mony mull horse, ilka ane on's beat deein' fat ae man - that's mysel' an' nae' ither - hed to dee maist single han' it'.

George Webster, a remarkable character, came across equally colourful folk on his travels.

There was James Lamb, a 'tailor bodie' from Muckle Wartle, who had his pocket picked by a 'coorse randie', Jane Greig.

Jeems, it seems. was 'an aul' creatur wi' blue knee-breeks an' ribbet hose, an' a red nichtcap on 's heid'.

It was said Jeems was a superstitious soul and frightened of 'bogles and boodies'. On a dark night he would pluck up courage by holding up his scissors in front of him, 'clip clippin' awa' at naething ava', 'as he hurried along a road.

Geordie's services would seem to have been indispensable, even with the arrival of the new police force. Fiscal Simpson was heard to say he would rather lose his horse and carriage that lose Geordie!

Geordie figured in two major cases. The 'pitifu'' story of John Booth we've already heard. I also touched on the brutal case of rape and murder at Auchterless. Quarryman James Robb, who worked at Tillymorgan, committed the crime after gaining entry to old Mary Smith's home by the chimney.

Robb left his stick at the scene, as well as a button from his velvet coat. When Geordie arrested Robb in his father's house in Fisherford the murderer's corduroy trousers were stained with soot.

Geordie arrested Robb on the spot and took him to Meldrum. They lodged that night at Badenscoth - 'we had plenty o' punch, an' a gweed fire i' the room'. While Geordie's colleague, Jock McCrae, stood guard at the bedside, the inimitable Webster took a cat-nap on the bed, with Robb at his side, their legs in irons.

At Oldmeldrum, folk turned out in force to gawp at the notorious prisoner. By the time Geordie and Robb reached Aberdeen it was getting late.

'The governor o' the jail wasna at han' bein' awa at some great meetin', an' I cudna get my prisoner gi'en owre. I was terrifiet to leave 'im oot o' my sicht till properly secur't, an' so I took 'im along to my ain lodgin's wi' Mrs McHardy, in the Adelphi, an' got redd o' him neist mornin', poor deevil'. Calcraft made his first appearance in Aberdeen in 1849, to hang Robb.

In the twilight of his life Geordie Webster said of his long and distinguished career: 'It was all done in the public interest, and for the public good; a terror to evildoers, and a protection to such as do well'.

George Webster died on March 1, 1883, at the age of 82. He is buried in Meldrum Parish Church, where in 1838 he nabbed the 'nickum Farquhar', who stole the kirk offering.

A granite slab marks the resting place of Geordie, his wife Margaret Rae, who predeceased him by almost four years, and four of their children, three of whom died in childhood.

Mary Webster, who died in May 1920, was the grandmother of Sime Halliday, one of Geordie's oldest surviving descendants. At 85, Mr Halliday still lives in his native Oldmeldrum. He is rightly proud of his famous ancestor, but admits he was a boy of 14 before he learned of his exploits.

He was in the town library one day when the local chemist handed him a slim volume. 'Here laddie', he said, 'take this book, you'll find if an interesting read'. It was Geordie Webster's autobiography.

Oldmeldrum's Sheriff and Criminal Officer George Webster, scourge of poachers and murderers.

Craiginches Prison, Aberdeen, photographed in 1934, the year child killer Jeannie Donald was due to hang in the jail. Her sentence was commuted to life imprisonment.

Chapter Nineteen

Rest Without Peace

Asmall granite cross with a poignant inscription was erected by the Dowager Lady Crawford in the grounds of Dunecht House in Aberdeenshire at the end of the last century.

It marks the spot where the body of her husband, Alexander, Earl of Crawford of Balcarres, lay hidden for 14 months after it was stolen from the vault in nearby Dunecht Chapel.

The Dunecht Mystery is an enduring enigma. There is no mystery about the reason for the heartless theft. The body was not stolen for medical research, but for financial gain.

But what puzzles criminologists today is - who was responsible? One man was convicted for the offence but at his trial the judge was of the strong opinion that more than two were implicated.

Similar outrages had been perpetrated - in the United States. In 1876 a gang was surprised in the act of stealing President Lincoln's body from his tomb. And two years later the corpse of a New York millionaire, Mr T.A. Stewart, was stolen and held to ransom. His widow offered a reward of 25,000 dollars but the body was never recovered.

The Earl of Crawford, a noted theologian, antiquarian and genealogist, with a love of astronomical research, died in Florence on December 13, 1880, during a year-long trip to Egypt and Italy.

His body was embalmed in Florence and placed in three coffins. The inner coffin was made of soft Italian wood. The middle one of lead and the outer one of highly-polished, carved oak and mounted with chased silver. The three coffins were deposited within a huge walnut shell, decorated with a cross. The total weight was almost half-a-ton!

The earl's body underwent a hazardous trip to Dunecht. First, it was transported across the Alps in the company of a faithful retainer, before being lashed to the deck of a chartered steamer for the Channel crossing. At Aberdeen no hearse could be found to carry the load, so the outer shell was removed. Scotland was swept by a violent snowstorm and the hearse was trapped behind drifts on its return from Dunecht.

The new mausoleum at Dunecht House had space for 64 coffins, but the earl's was the first. The heavy outer shell was deposited in the vault beside the three coffins in which the body was encased.

The white-marbled mortuary chapel had not been consecrated at the time of the earl's death so the Bishop of Aberdeen performed the rite before the interment on December 29, 1880. The coffin was manhandled into place by eight men.

Access to the vault was by a short flight of eight steps. The steps and stairway were covered by four slabs of Caithness granite and sealed.

But on the morning of Thursday, December 1, 1881 - almost a year later - labourer William Hadden stumbled upon the macabre mystery of Dunecht. A layer of mould had been shovelled off the flagstones and a granite flagstone, weighing 15 hundredweights, concealing the entrance of the tomb, had been uprooted.

The estate commissioner William Yeats, an Aberdeen advocate, was informed and he hurried to Dunecht House, 12 miles away, accompanied by Inspector George Cran of Aberdeen County Police. They were joined by the Echt bobby, Constable John Robb.

On descending the stairs they found the vault in disarray. Iron bars and heavy planks lay on the steps. The floor of the vault was strewn with planks and sawdust which emitted a strong scent.

But worst of all the three coffins had been crudely opened and rifled. And the earl's body was missing! Because of the state of the sawdust and the leaden shell, where hacked, was oxidised, it was clear the work had taken place some months before.

Even as Inspector Cran arranged for all estate workers to be interviewed, Mr Yeats handed him a nasty surprise - the estate commissioner had been told of the theft three months earlier!

He showed the policeman a letter he had received on September 8. It was anonymous and bore an Aberdeen postmark.

'Sir, - The remains of the late Earl of Crawford are not beneath the chaple (sic) at Dunecht as you believe, but were removed hence last spring, and the smell of decayed flowers ascending from the vault since that time will, on investigation, be found to proceed from another cause than flowers. NABOB.'

On receipt of this odd letter Yeats spoke to the man who had constructed the vault. They dismissed the letter as a cruel hoax, but at least had the sense to file it.

Other pieces of the jig-saw fell into place after the crime came to light. It was recalled how the previous May, five months after the earl's interment, members of the staff reported a pleasant aromatic smell wafting from the vault. It was thought to be the odour of decaying wreaths, as outlined in Nabob's letter. Masons filled in cracks around the flagstones, believing frost caused the damage, and then as a finishing touch estate gardeners spread soil over the flags. Grass was sown and shrubs and flowers planted. An iron railing was added.

The Dunecht Mystery baffled and outraged the country. Queen Victoria sent an 'expression of sympathy' to the new peer and his family.

The Aberdeen 'Evening Express' thundered: 'Body-lifting, though common enough in this as in other districts some fifty years ago, is a crime now almost unknown; and the horror raised by this sacrilegious act is, if anything, deepened by the skill, patience and mastery villainy that seems to have been brought to bear in its conception and execution'.

As wild rumours swept Aberdeen and North-east Scotland about the reasons behind the macabre theft, 100 policemen and estate workers scoured the Dunecht Estate, without luck.

It was suspected that a person with inside knowledge of the estate was the culprit (hence the reference to decaying wreaths?) and that he had more than one accomplice.

The earl's family offered a £50 reward for further information on 'Nabob', while a bloodhound Morgan, who had located the remains of a child in an infamous Blackburn murder case, was brought in by the police, but preferred chasing rabbits in Dunecht Woods!

Eventually 'Nabob' got in touch with the earl's London solicitor and said the body was still in Aberdeenshire although he had no wish to be *assinated by rusarectionests nor suspected by the public of being an accomplice in such dastardly work*.

Amateur crimebusters and local clairvoyants got in on the act, much to the annoyance of the police, but there was no trace of the missing body.

The family took the Home Secretary's advice and refused to offer a reward for the recovery of the body. But a £600 reward

(£500 by the family and £100 by the Government) and a free pardon to any accomplice other than the perpetrator, for information leading to the arrest of the culprit, was announced.

In February 1882 two men were arrested in connection with the affair but the suspected persons, Thomas Kirkwood, a joiner at Dunecht Estate, and John Philip, a shoemaker, and one time drill instructor at the Echt Volunteer Corps, were later discharged.

For five months public interest waned, then the police, acting on a tip-off, arrested Charles Soutar, a 42-year-old vermin catcher, of Donald's Court (now the site of a public house) in Aberdeen's Schoolhill.

Soutar had been employed for five to six years as a rat catcher by the Dunecht Estate but had been sacked for poaching three years before the earl died.

The police informant was Aberdeen game dealer George Machray, who had been a gamekeeper at Ury House, Stonehaven, when the prisoner was employed as a rat catcher there. Soutar had tried to get Machray to act as a go-between with the late earl's agent so that he 'could tell where the body was on two conditions, namely that they would find out the persons who took the body, and give protection to him'. Machray later reported Soutar to the police.

On the same day Soutar was judicially examined by Sheriff Comrie Thomson in Aberdeen. Soutar admitted writing the Nabob letters.

On being asked: 'What do you know of the removal of the late Earl of Crawford's body', Soutar revealed an astonishing story.

Soutar claimed that while poaching in Crow Wood, near Dunecht House, one night in April or May 1881, he was confronted by a group of men, their faces blackened or hidden by masks. Two of the men were 'young-like chaps, of middle size', who spoke in a common Aberdeenshire accent. Their two companions seemed to be 'gentlemen', with the taller of this pair apparently the leader of the gang. Soutar claimed he was threatened with a pistol, but he was recognised as being a poacher.

Soutar was told that if he had been a spy he would not have seen the light of another day. 'Remember what I am going to tell you', the leader said. 'You're known to our party, and if you breathe a syllable of what you have seen, I will have your life if you're on the face of the earth'.

The poacher returned to the spot at daybreak and found a man's body wrapped in a blanket. At the time he thought the man had been murdered. He detected the smell of benzoline and thought they had tried to destroy the corpse. Soutar refused to tell the police where the body could be found. 'I'll rather wait until you get them that took the body; it will be safer for me then'.

The police renewed their efforts and on Tuesday, July 18, 1882, the earl's body was found swathed in blankets in a shallow grave, 500 yards from the window of his favourite study at Dunecht House.

Soutar stuck to his weird tale when he stood trial at the High Court of Justiciary in Edinburgh, on Monday, October 23, 1882, charged with violating the sepulchres of the dead and the raising and carrying away dead bodies out of their graves.

Lord Craighill, in his summing up to the jury, said: 'It was perfectly impossible that one man alone could accomplish what had been done; probably more than two were concerned. The vault was opened and closed the same night without suspicion being aroused, and not only strength but skill was employed in the perpetration of this offence. The body was removed, the grave was dug, and all traces of these operations were obliterated. Probably these things were not all done on a single night, and certainly one man could not have done them; there must have been others. The guilt of the prisoner, however, if he were concerned, was in law the same as if he had been the sole offender'.

Soutar, the body-snatching rat-catcher, was found guilty after a two-day trial and sentenced to five years' penal servitude.

In the words of the Dean of Faculty, the Dunecht Mystery was only half solved by the jury's verdict.

The reward money was cut in half because it was certain Soutar was not the only person implicated in the crime. The £300 went to Machray.

Soutar still pleaded his innocence on his release from prison.

The Earl of Crawford's body was finally laid to rest in the Lindsay family vault at Wigan after the town council gave permission for it to be reopened after quarter-a-century.

The crypt at Dunecht House, the home of Viscount Cowdray, now serves as a garage.

Chapter Twenty

'Nellfield Pies'

Horror gripped Victorian Aberdeen in the summer of 1899 as ghoulish revelations emanated from a West End graveyard.

A gravedigger with a grudge against the superintendent of Nellfield Cemetery had turned informer.

At six o'clock on a bright morning uniformed police, detectives and workmen with picks, shovels and bulky ledgers, descended on the high-walled graveyard to get to the bottom of the grisly allegations.

What they discovered was a sickening scandal which the medical journal, 'The Lancet', recorded at the time, 'produced much mental disquietude among lairholders, at least one of whom has died from excitement'.

In the next few days of early June the so-called 'probers' - men carrying iron rods - and diggers realised that scores of graves had been tampered with, with the contents heartlessly exhumed and destroyed in most cases.

At the eye of the storm was William Coutts, the cemetery superintendent, who, because of the infamy of the case, spent six weeks in Craiginches Prison, Aberdeen, more or less for his own good, before being allowed out on bail.

Coutts was employed by the Aberdeen Baker Incorporation, the graveyard trustees, and it was his zeal that led to gravediggers emptying the older lairs to make room for fresh interments. Unlike the body-snatchers of the earlier era the gold lay in the lairs, and not the corpses.

Four months before the scandal broke the Harvey family of Aberdeen sought interim interdict against the trustees and Coutts from interfering with their relatives' resting place. The revelations that day gave a hint of the horrors to come.

It came to a head after an employee blew the whistle on Coutts. The superintendent was arrested and charged with violating a sepulchre and perjury, arising from the Harvey civil action. On the day the scandal broke his employers advertised in the 'Aberdeen Journal' for a new superintendent at £700 a year with a free house.

It was just as well Coutts was behind bars at Craiginches. The exhumation teams found decaying bodies crammed below footpaths in Nellfield Cemetery. Bits of bodies had been burned in the toolhouse furnace. A pit contained 400 coffin handles and ashes. In one lair alone there had been 29 burials inside three months!

Crowds flocked to the graveyard at the foot of Great Western Road.

In one evening, thousands of people, some weeping and wearing black, swept through the burial ground, gawking at the violated tombs or anxiously checking a loved one's last resting place.

In the early stages of the police inquiries a guard was placed on the cemetery gates. Onlookers were kept at bay. One enterprising reporter joined a group of mourners at a funeral and was able to get into the cemetery to witness police at work. Urchins were seen 'stealing along the distant wall and dodging behind the chimney cans of wash houses in the hope of evading the eagle eye of the guardians of the peace'.

The Press had a field day. The 'Aberdeen Journal' had an active 'army of newsboys', and snapped up all available horse cabs to distribute the newspaper throughout the city.

Relic-hunting and vandalism were unsuccessfully discouraged.

The Nellfield Cemetery Scandal shocked the nation. The 'Pall Mall Gazette' thundered: 'The body-snatching of an earlier day was scarcely equal to this'.

'The News of the World' observed: 'The reports from Aberdeen rival the stories of Burke and Hare in gruesomeness and horror. They indicate that no respect whatsoever has been paid to the sanctity of the tomb'.

It warned: 'There is too much reason to fear that Aberdeen is not the only centre where such ghoulish performances take place, and the investigations may tend to reveal similar scandals in other places'.

Questions about the affair were raised in Parliament.

In Aberdeen the factor of Nellfield Cemetery was mobbed by stick-wielding youths chanting: 'Burn the bodies!' and 'Nellfield scoundrel!', and his baker's shop in Chapel Street was boycotted.

When Coutts was smuggled out of jail by coach a cat-calling mob chased it, screaming: 'Nellfield pies!', which gives a hint of the sort of rumours sweeping the Granite City. Even so, Coutts, prior to his trial, was reported to be 'remarkably well and in good spirits' when reunited with his family at their home in Ferryhill Terrace.

The scandal reached its climax in late September 1899 when Coutts appeared in the dock at the High Court in Aberdeen. The only light relief in a harrowing trial came at the very start when Coutts was summoned to the dock and a juryman with the same name answered.

The trial ended with a whimper, rather than a bang. On the fourth day, a Saturday, Coutts changed his plea to guilty of seven charges.

By then it was realised Coutts was no Victorian Burker. He had no sordid personal motive in his gruesome work. Nor had he been in it for personal financial gain. The truth appeared to be that he had been eager to please his bosses, although, they of course, were totally ignorant of his business methods.

Lord McLaren jailed Coutts for six months.

Coutts was out of a job, but his bosses had already picked his successor from the 60 applicants from all over the country!

Chapter Twenty-one

Infamous Last Words

In December 1864 a Port Elphinstone timber merchant George Stephen smashed his paramour's skull with an axe at their trysting place in the woods at Thainstone, south of Inverurie.

Sixty-two-year-old Stephen pleaded guilty to the murder of Aberdeen woman Ann Forbes. But because it was decided he was insane at the time of the crime he was reprieved four days before he was due to hang in Aberdeen.

When the Lord Provost, accompanied by magistrates and jail officials, went to break the good news, Stephen betrayed no emotion. In reply to a question as to whether he knew what it all meant a stony-faced Stephen said:

'Ou, aye - jist a whilie langer to live!'

Farmworker Robert Smith, incarcerated in Peterhead Prison for murdering a workmate near Stonehaven in 1893, was equally ungrateful when told a petition might be organised to mitigate his life sentence.

'Dae nae such thing', he fumed. 'I was never so happy and comfortable all my life. The meat is guid and aye sure, and ye ha'e a roof abune your heid. It's far better than howin' neeps or howkin' tatties!'

Epilogue

By a weird, chilling coincidence places forever associated with Aberdeen's 'Black Kalendar' are linked to four of the city's most infamous crimes of the 20th century.

In May 1963 a young labourer Henry John Burnett, 'Harry' to his friends and family, blasted off a shotgun at his girlfriend's husband.

Burnett, who was 21, went to the gallows in Craiginches Prison on August 15, after being found guilty of capital murder at an Aberdeen High Court trial.

The murder took place in a flat in Jackson Terrace, next to the lane, which in the 18th century, formed the track that led to the gibbet on Gallow Hill. After the shooting Burnett fled up this lane. He hijacked a car within a short distance of the old execution site and was recaptured at Ellon after a police chase.

In a flat in Urquhart Road, just around the corner from Gallow Hill, Jeannie Donald murdered the wee daughter of an upstairs neighbour in April 1934. It was a crime that shocked the nation.

Donald vigorously denied the charge but scientific evidence led by Professor Sydney Smith, of the Chair of Forensic Evidence at Edinburgh University, proved she had indeed murdered eight-year-old Helen Priestly.

Donald was found guilty by an Edinburgh jury and was sentenced to hang in Craiginches Prison on August 13, but this was later commuted to life imprisonment.

Aberdeen was shocked by two child murders in the early 1960s.

In July 1963 a seven-year-old boy vanished from his home in Justice Street. A wide-scale search was mounted and it was feared the lad had drowned. A boy, similar in appearance to the missing child, had been seen playing in the harbour area, and on rocks at the beach.

Four months later the boy's body was exhumed from the floor of a greenhouse, a few hundred yards from his family home.

The allotment holder, Wick-born James Oliphant, who lived in attic 'digs' above a bank in Aberdeen's Market Street, was arrested. He would later admit to killing the boy, and a little Woodside girl, whose brutal murder in January 1961 had baffled police.

On account of Oliphant's mental condition the murder charges were later reduced to culpable homicide and in February 1964 he was detained for life in Carstairs State Hospital, where he later died.

The allotment which Oliphant tended was situated on Heading Hill, where they burned witches and beheaded criminals, and no distance from the site of 'Hangman's Brae'.

Bibliography

Adams, Norman - *Dead and Buried? The Horrible History of Bodysnatching (1972)*

Adams, Norman - *In the Dead of Night! (1990)*

Anderson, Robert - *Aberdeen in Bygone Days (1910)*

Carnie, William - *Reporting Reminiscences (three volumes)*

Chambers, Robert - *Traditions of Edinburgh (1980)*

Dickinson, W.C. - *Early Records of the Burgh of Aberdeen, 1398-1407 (1957)*

Fraser, G.M. - *Aberdeen Street Names (1911, updated 1986)*

Fraser, G.M. - *Historical Aberdeen (1905)*

Gordon, George - *The Shore Porters Society of Aberdeen, 1498-1969*

Gordon, George - *Prying with the Pynours, 1498-1978*

Grant, James - *Cassell's Old and New Edinburgh*

Hobbs, Alexander - *Downie's Slaughter - Aberdeen University Review, 1973-74*

Irvine, Hamish - *The Diced Cap, The Story of Aberdeen City Police (1972)*

Keith, Alexander - *A Thousand Years of Aberdeen (1972)*

Keith, Alexander - *Eminent Aberdonians (1984)*

Kennedy, William - *Annals of Aberdeen (1818)*

Lynch, Michael, Michael Spearman and Geoffrey Stell - *The Scottish Medieval Town (1985)*

Lumsden, Louisa Innes - *Memories of Aberdeen a Hundred years Ago (1927, reprinted 1988)*

Millar, A.H. - *Haunted Dundee (1923)*

Milne, John - *Aberdeen (1911)*

Mackinnon, Lachlan - *Recollections of an Old Lawyer (1935)*

McPherson, J.M. - *Primitive Beliefs in the North-east of Scotland (1929)*

Rayner, J.L. & Crook, G.T. - *The Complete Newgate Calender (1926)*

131

Rettie, James - *Aberdeen Fifty Years Ago (1868, republished as Aberdeen 150 Years Ago (1972))*

Robbie, William - *Aberdeen; Traditions and History (1893)*

Robertson, Joseph - *The Black Kalendar of Aberdeen (1871)*

Robertson, Joseph - *The Book of Bon-Accord (1839)*

Roughead, William - *Twelve Scots Trials (1913)*

Roughead, William - *Knave's Looking Glass (1935)*

Roughead, William - *The Riddle of the Ruthvens (1936)*

Skene, William - *East Neuk Chronicles (1905)*

Stark, James - *Dr Kidd of Aberdeen (1896)*

Smith, Lewis - *Autographic Notes and Comments 1807-1880 (unpublished)*

Taylor, Louise B. - *Aberdeen Council Letters (Vol. 1), 1559-1633 (1942)*

Thom, Walter - *History of Aberdeen (1811)*

Turreff, Gavin - *Antiquarian Gleanings (1859)*

Webster, George - *Criminal Officer of the Old School (1880)*

Whittington-Egan, Richard - *William Roughead's Chronicles of Murder (1991)*

Wilson, Robert - *The Book of Bon-Accord (1822)*

Wyness, Fenton - *City by the Grey North Sea: Aberdeen (1965)*

Wyness, Fenton - *More Spots from the Leopard (1971)*

Twenty-One Aberdeen Events of the Nineteenth Century (1912)

A Tale of Two Burghs - The Archaeology of Old and New Aberdeen (1987)

The Miscellany of the Spalding Club (Volumes One and Five)

The Scots Black Kalendar - (1938, new edition 1985)

A Report of the Trial of Malcolm Gillespie and George Skene Edwards for Forgery (1827)

Aberdeen Journal Notes and Queries - Volume III (1910)

The Life and Remarkable Adventures of Peter Young, the Famous Caird (1867)

Periodicals:
Aberdeen Chronicle, Aberdeen Herald, Aberdeen Journal, Aberdeen Leopard, Aberdeen Observer, The Deeside Field, Weekly News.

Acknowledgements

The author would gratefully like to acknowledge the guidance and help of many people, particularly Miss Judith Cripps, Aberdeen City Archivist, Mr William Moir, of Aberdeen City Architect's Division, Mr I.R. Douglas of Dunecht Estates, and the staffs of the University of Aberdeen Library (Department of Special Collections and Archives), and the City Arts and Recreation Libraries Division at Schoolhill and Woodside. I would also like to thank Norman Adams, of Aberdeen City Council's Publicity and Promotions Division, for the use of the photographs of Aberdeen Tolbooth.